PENGUIN BOOKS

RECOLLECTIONS OF MY NONEXISTENCE

Rebecca Solnit is the author of more than twenty books, including *A Field Guide to Getting Lost*, *The Faraway Nearby*, *A Paradise Built in Hell*, *River of Shadows*, and *Wanderlust*. She is also the author of *Men Explain Things to Me* and many essays on feminism, activism, and social change, hope, and the climate crisis. A product of the California public education system from kindergarten to graduate school, she is a regular contributor to *The Guardian* and other publications.

* * *

Praise for *Recollections of My Nonexistence*

"Much more than a feminist manifesto . . . Solnit movingly describes her efforts to fashion 'the self who will speak' . . . There are phrases, such as 'women's stories,' 'silencing,' or 'gaslighting,' that contemporary discourse has emptied out. Solnit revives these terms with the breath of their own histories."　—Katy Waldman, *The New Yorker*

"Throughout her rich body of work, essayist and critic Rebecca Solnit has revealed pieces of herself in writings about the beauty of getting lost, the joys of walking both for pleasure and with purpose, and perhaps most famously, the indignity of being mansplained to. At last, she uses her eagle eye to explore her own life. *Recollections of My Nonexistence* is a marvel: a memoir that details her awakening as a feminist, an environmentalist, and a citizen of the world. Every single sentence is exquisite."　—Maris Kreizman, *Vulture*

"A clarion call of a memoir, chronicling, in unfettered, poetic prose, her coming-of-age . . . and her emergence as one of our most potent cultural critics."　—O, *The Oprah Magazine*

"For Solnit fans, her new memoir is a glimpse of all that was 'taking form out of sight,' providing a key to understanding much of her work to date. Yet simply as a coming-of-age narrative, it also has much to offer someone new to her writing. [*Recollections*] often reverses the figure-ground relationship, portraying the emergence of a writer and her voice from a particular cultural moment and set of fortuitous influences. . . . [It] often reads as a letter to young activists and women writers—less 'back in my day' and more 'I fought, and am fighting, the same battles you are.'"

—Jenny Odell, *The New York Times Book Review*

"A deeply intimate and deeply internal book about how Solnit became one of the defining feminist thinkers of the twenty-first century [and] a nostalgic love letter to the San Francisco of her youth. . . . Solnit writes beautifully and with much compassionate nuance about how the threat of violence and not just its execution colors all parts of a woman's life, and how actual physical violence is just one of myriad ways that women are controlled, subjugated and silenced."

—*San Francisco Chronicle*

"Solnit has valiantly been making the case that misogynist speech and violence are on a spectrum for decades, long before mainstream acceptance of the idea. . . . In *Recollections of My Nonexistence*, Solnit implies that just as the illness can be both dramatic and also cumulative, gradual, and imperceptible, so might be the cure. And things that feel insufficient—writing, talking, walking, teaching—do in fact represent tiny counterweights, which together shift the course of culture."

—NPR.org

"*Recollections of My Nonexistence* is a powerful examination of the way small moments can accumulate in a brilliant mind to formulate big ideas and even help conceive a better world." —*Los Angeles Times*

"Solnit emphasizes the need to find poetry in survival. . . . [*Recollections of My Nonexistence* is] a voice raised in hope against gender violence. It's a call we should listen to."   —*The Washington Post*

"It is a rare writer who has both the intellectual heft and the authority of frontline experience to tackle the most urgent issues of our time. One of the reasons [Solnit] has won so many admirers is the sense that she is driven not by anger but by compassion and the desire to offer encouragement. . . . That voice of hope is more essential now than ever, and this memoir is a valuable glimpse into the grit and courage that enabled her to keep telling sidelined stories."

—*The Guardian* (London)

"A work of feminist solidarity, in which [Solnit] chooses to write not from herself alone, but 'for and about and often with the voices of other women talking about survival.' . . . What Solnit wants most is to talk about the obstacles her younger self found. . . . She's concerned with the way women disappear, or are encouraged to abdicate their bodies and their vocation. . . . [A] meditation on creativity, home, and an elusive self."   —*4Columns*

"[A] splendid memoir of longings and determinations, of resistances and revolutions, personal and political, illuminating the kiln in which one of the boldest, most original minds of our time was annealed."

—Maria Popova, *BrainPickings*

"One of the more beautiful narratives I've read."   —Ezra Klein, *Vox*

"Rebecca Solnit's opposition to injustice in its many forms, and her relentless inquiry as a writer and reporter into a great range of issues— racial injustice, nuclear weapons, indigenous rights, male hegemony— have defined the outrage and politics of much of her generation. In

Recollections of My Nonexistence she draws all these potent metaphors for inequity together into a moral stance that transcends the particulars of all her topics. This is a remarkable book—smart, brave, edgy, insightful, and authentic."

—Barry Lopez

"One of our foremost thinkers on womanhood explores the journey of her becoming in this deeply personal memoir about her youth in San Francisco. In her searing, sensitive voice, Solnit recalls the epidemic of violence against women . . . tracing her journey as a writer through her journey to speak out on behalf of women."

—*Esquire*

"Activist and essayist Rebecca Solnit has long captured the discomforts and difficulties of modern womanhood. . . . In describing [her youth], she details how she found her voice as an advocate for herself and those around her."

—*Time*

"[Solnit] couches her own lived experience . . . within a larger exploration of contemporary womanhood and an unapologetically feminist, queer lens. While beautifully exercising her own literary voice, Solnit simultaneously poses the question: Who do we allow to characterize the female experience? And what needs to happen in order for that to change?"

—*Parade*

"An inquisitive, perceptive, and original thinker and enthralling writer . . . Solnit has created an unconventional and galvanizing memoir-in-essays that shares key, often terrifying, formative moments in her valiant writing life . . . [and] illuminates with piercing lyricism the body-and-soul dangers women face in our complexly, violently misogynist world. . . . An incandescent addition to the literature of dissent and creativity."

—*Booklist* (starred review)

ALSO BY REBECCA SOLNIT

Recollections
of My
Nonexistence

‧--‧◆‧--‧

Rebecca Solnit

PENGUIN BOOKS

PENGUIN BOOKS

An imprint of Penguin Random House LLC
penguinrandomhouse.com

First published in the United States of America by Viking,
an imprint of Penguin Random House LLC, 2020
Published in Penguin Books 2021

Copyright © 2020 by Rebecca Solnit
Penguin supports copyright. Copyright fuels creativity, encourages diverse
voices, promotes free speech, and creates a vibrant culture. Thank you for
buying an authorized edition of this book and for complying with copyright
laws by not reproducing, scanning, or distributing any part of it in any form
without permission. You are supporting writers and allowing Penguin to
continue to publish books for every reader.

Frontispiece courtesy of the author

Grateful acknowledgment is made for permission to reprint the following:

Excerpt from "Never Before," [*The New Yorker*, 1980] reprinted with
permission of Frances Levine.

"Rant" by Diane di Prima, from *Pieces of a Song*. Copyright © 1990 by Diane di
Prima. Reprinted with the permission of City Lights Books, www.citylights.com.

ISBN 9780593083345 (paperback)

THE LIBRARY OF CONGRESS HAS CATALOGED THE
HARDCOVER EDITION AS FOLLOWS:
Names: Solnit, Rebecca, author.
Title: Recollections of my nonexistence / Rebecca Solnit.
Identifiers: LCCN 2019022497 (print) | LCCN 2019022498 (ebook) |
ISBN 9780593083338 (hardcover) | ISBN 9780593083352 (ebook)
Subjects: LCSH: Solnit, Rebecca. | Women authors,
American—20th century—Biography.
Classification: LCC PS3569.O585 Z46 2020 (print) |
LCC PS3569.O585 (ebook) | DDC 814/.54 [B]—dc23
LC record available at https://lccn.loc.gov/2019022497
LC ebook record available at https://lccn.loc.gov/2019022498

Printed in the United States of America
1   3   5   7   9   10   8   6   4   2

Set in Adobe Jenson Pro
Designed by Cassandra Garruzzo

Contents

Looking Glass House

One day long ago, I looked at myself as I faced a full-length mirror and saw my image darken and soften and then seem to retreat, as though I was vanishing from the world rather than that my mind was shutting it out. I steadied myself on the door frame just across the hall from the mirror, and then my legs crumpled under me. My own image drifted away from me into darkness, as though I was only a ghost fading even from my own sight.

I blacked out occasionally and had dizzy spells often in those days, but this time was memorable because it appeared as though it wasn't that the world was vanishing from my consciousness but that I was vanishing from the world. I was the person who was vanishing and the disembodied person watching her from a distance, both and neither. In those days, I was trying to disappear and to appear, trying to be safe and to be someone, and those agendas were often at odds with each other. And I was watching myself to see if I could read in the mirror what I could be and whether I was good enough and whether all the things I'd been told about myself were true.

To be a young woman is to face your own annihilation in innumerable ways or to flee it or the knowledge of it, or all these things at once. "The death of a beautiful woman is, unquestionably, the most poetical topic in the world," said Edgar Allan Poe, who must not have imagined it from the perspective of women who prefer to live. I was trying not to be the subject of someone else's poetry and not to get killed; I was trying to find a poetics of my own, with no maps, no guides, not much to go on. They might have been out there, but I hadn't located them yet.

The struggle to find a poetry in which your survival rather than your defeat is celebrated, perhaps to find your own voice to insist upon that, or to at least find a way to survive amidst an ethos that relishes your erasures and failures is work that many and perhaps most young women have to do. In those early years, I did not do it particularly well or clearly, but I did it ferociously.

I was often unaware of what and why I was resisting, and so my defiance was murky, incoherent, erratic. Those years of not succumbing, or of succumbing like someone sinking into a morass and then flailing to escape, again and again, come back to me now as I see young women around me fighting the same battles. The fight wasn't just to survive bodily, though that could be intense enough, but to survive as a person possessed of rights, including the right to participation and dignity and a voice. More than survive, then: to live.

The director, writer, and actor Brit Marling said recently, "Part of what keeps you sitting in that chair in that room enduring harassment or abuse from a man in power is that, as a woman, you have rarely seen another end for yourself. In the novels you've read, in the films you've seen, in the stories you've been told since birth, the women so frequently meet disastrous ends."

The mirror in which I saw myself disappear was in the apartment I inhabited for a quarter century, beginning in the last months of my teens. The first several years there were the era of my fiercest battles, some of which I won, some of which left scars I still carry, many of which so formed me that I cannot say I wish that it had all been otherwise, for then I would have been someone else entirely, and she does not exist. I do. But I can wish that the young women who come after me might skip some of the old obstacles, and some of my writing has been toward that end, at least by naming those obstacles.

2

nother mirror story: When I was about eleven there was a shoe store where my mother got me the engineer boots I favored back when I was trying not to be that despised thing, a girl, and was trying to be what seemed like a separate thing, rugged, ready for action, but something else made the store memorable. If you stepped in front of the mirrors that lined both sides of the center aisle, you could see an image of an image of an image of an image of yourself or the shoe stools or anything, each one more watery and dim and remote, stretching onward, beyond, seemingly forever, as though an ocean lay in there with the reflections and you were seeing farther and farther into the sea-green depths. It wasn't the self I was trying to catch sight of then, but the beyond.

Beyond every beginning is another beginning, and another and another, but my first ride, eight years later, on the 5 Fulton bus could be a place to start, that bus line that bisects the city, running from downtown, by San Francisco Bay, all the way west out Fulton Street to the Pacific Ocean. The main thrust of this story happens in the middle of that route, in the middle of the city, but for just a moment stay on the bus straining uphill past the Jesuit church whose towers catch the morning light, onward alongside the big park on the south side of the street and avenue after avenue of houses less and less densely packed on earth that is really only sand, to that sandy stretch meeting the Pacific Ocean that covers almost a third of the planet.

Sometimes the whole sea looks like a mirror of beaten silver, though it's too turbulent to hold many reflections; it's the bay that carries a reflected sky on its surface. On the most beautiful days, there are no words for the colors of San Francisco Bay and the sky above it. Sometimes the water reflects a heaven that is both gray and gold, and the water is blue, is green, is silver, is a mirror of that gray and gold, catching the warmth and cold of colors in its ripples, is all and none of them, is something more subtle than the language we have. Sometimes a bird dives into the mirror of the water, vanishing into its own reflection, and the reflective surface makes it impossible to see what lies beneath.

Sometimes at the birth and death of a day, the opal sky is no color we have words for, the gold shading into blue without the intervening green that is halfway between those colors, the fiery warm colors that are not apricot or crimson or gold, the light morphing second by second so that the sky is more shades of blue than you can count as it fades from where the sun is to the far side where other colors are happening. If you look away for a moment you miss a shade for which there will never be a term, and it is transformed into another and another. The names of the colors are sometimes cages containing what doesn't belong there, and this is often true of language generally, of the words like *woman, man, child, adult, safe, strong, free, true, black, white, rich, poor.* We need the words, but use them best knowing they are containers forever spilling over and breaking open. Something is always beyond.

ometimes a gift is given and neither giver nor recipient knows what its true dimensions are, and what it appears to be at first is not what it will be in the end. Like beginnings, endings have endless recessions, layers atop the layers, consequences that ripple outward. One winter Sunday when I was young, ignorant, poor, and almost friendless, I went to look at an apartment for rent. I'd found the listing in the want ads of the newspaper, a few tiny lines of information in that dense gray grid, mostly describing places out of my range. People had laughed at me when I'd said I was looking for something for $200 a month, a rock-bottom price even then, but I couldn't afford any more that last semester of my undergraduate education, that third year of my financial independence.

At the time I went house hunting I lived in a tiny room with a window onto a light shaft that was nevertheless luxurious for having its own bathroom in that residential hotel whose other rooms had shared bathrooms down the hall. The entire building shared a single dimly lit kitchen where your food would be stolen from the refrigerator or swarmed over by roaches or both. The other residents were people whose lives seemed to have not turned out well. I was nineteen and my life had not turned out yet; I was still early in the process of trying to figure out who and how to become, the usual task for someone that age. (I had taken the GED at fifteen and started community college full time at sixteen, transferring to a four-year college at seventeen; at nineteen I was a senior at San Francisco State University, the working-class college out in the windy southwest corner of the city.)

I got on the 5 Fulton near city hall and the bus took me past the housing projects, past a Fillmore Street church where a group of somber black men in suits were gathered outside for a funeral, past ornate old wooden houses and corner liquor stores, up a rise to Lyon Street, where I stepped off, and the bus lumbered on to the Pacific. I found the address, a building with a recessed front door that had, like a lot of the others nearby, an ironwork gate added for more security. The doormat inside was attached to the mail slot with a rusty chain and lock. I rang the manager's doorbell, trudged up the first flight of stairs when he buzzed me in, and met him at the doorway of his apartment on the second floor, from which he dispatched me to the third floor to see the apartment directly above his.

The place astonished me with its beauty. A corner studio whose main room had a south and an east bay window through which light cascaded. Golden oak floors, high coved ceilings, and white walls with rectangular panels of molding. Glass-paneled doors with crystal doorknobs. A separate kitchen with another east-facing window that would explode with morning light when the

sun came up over the big house across the street. It seemed luminous, a little unearthly, a place from a fairy tale, immense and exquisite compared to the spartan single rooms in which I'd mostly
lived since I'd left home shortly after I turned seventeen. I floated
around in it for a while, then went back downstairs and told the
manager I wanted it. He said, kindly, "If you want it you should
have it." I wanted it passionately; it was more beautiful than anything I'd ever dreamed I could have, and being in it seemed like a
dream itself.

He was a big black man of sixty, tall, stout, strong, clearly once
very handsome, still an impressive figure with a low, rumbling
voice, and if he was dressed that day as he was most days I knew
him, he was probably wearing overalls. He brought me into his par-
lor. That Super Bowl Sunday afternoon when a local football team
was in the game and a roar would go up from homes throughout
the neighborhood with every score, he was watching black men
play the blues on his big TV sitting on its own table near the six-
sided green-felt poker table, the light outside filtered through old-
fashioned wide-slatted blinds over his bay windows. When he
handed me the rental application, my heart fell. I told him that I
had already been turned down by the slumlord management company whose name was at the top of the form. One of the employees
had disdainfully dropped my application into the wastebasket next
to his desk while I looked on; I didn't make enough money to meet
their minimums.

The building manager told me that if I got a respectable older
woman to apply, he wouldn't tell them of the deception. I took
up that offer and asked my mother, who had often refused to go
out on a limb for me, if she would. This time she did, filling out and

submitting the form. The management company was not suspicious about why a white homeowner who lived on the other side of the Golden Gate Bridge wanted the apartment—I think she said something about being closer to work, because she kept the books in a talent agency in the city. They probably gave it to her by rote as the most financially impressive applicant for a small place in a black neighborhood.

For the next eight years, I paid my rent every month by buying a money order and signing her name rather than mine to it. The lease specified that the person who'd signed it be the person who lived there, so I did not officially exist in my home that was not officially mine. Though I would end up spending so many years there, I felt for a long time that I might be chased off at any time and should be as invisible as possible, which reinforced a tendency toward furtiveness, a habit of trying to go undetected, that I'd developed as a child. At some point, the property management company found out that the resident was not the signer of the lease and asked the building manager what was going on. He vouched for me as a quiet, responsible tenant, and nothing happened, but I still felt precarious.

James V. Young was the building manager's name. I always called him Mr. Young. Sometime or other he mentioned that I was the first white person to live in the building in seventeen years. The other residents were mostly older couples, though a single mother and her friendly daughter lived in another one of the studio apartments in that building, which had seven apartments opening off the stairwell on two stories, above a ground floor of garages. That I had moved into a black neighborhood was something I had not yet grasped; it would teach me many things over the years to come, and

I would stay so long that when I left, I left a middle-class white place whose buildings remained largely unchanged beyond fresh paint, but where everything else was transformed and something vital had died.

I changed too; the person who moved out in the twenty-first century was not that person who'd arrived all those years before. There is a thread of continuity. The child is mother of the woman, but so much happened, so much changed, that I think of that spindly, anxious young woman as someone I knew intimately, someone I wish I could have done more for, someone I feel for as I often do for the women her age I meet now; that long-ago person was not exactly me, not like me at all in crucial ways, but me anyway, an awkward misfit, a daydreamer, a restless wanderer.

The word *adult* implies that all the people who've attained legal majority make up a coherent category, but we are travelers who change and traverse a changing country as we go. The road is tattered and elastic. Childhood fades gradually in some ways, never ends in others; adulthood arrives in small, irregular installments if it arrives; and every person is on her own schedule, or rather there is none for the many transitions. When you leave home, if you had one, when you start out on your own, you're someone who was a child for most of her life, though even what it means to be a child is ill-defined.

Some people have others who will tend and fund and sometimes confine them all their lives, some people are gradually weaned, some of us are cut off abruptly and fend for ourselves, some always did. Still, out on your own, you're a new immigrant to the nation of adults, and the customs are strange: you're learning to hold together all the pieces of a life, figure out what that life is going to be and who is going to be part of it, and what you will do with your self-determination.

You are in your youth walking down a long road that will branch and branch again, and your life is full of choices with huge and unpredictable consequences, and you rarely get to come back to choose the other route. You are making something, a life, a self, and it is an intensely creative task as well as one at which it is more than possible to fail, a little, a lot, miserably, fatally. Youth is a high-risk business. Once, around the time I moved into Mr. Young's building, I was approached as I walked across a plaza near city hall by members of a cult. In the early 1980s, the cults that had done so much damage through the 1970s had yet to fade away. They seemed to be the consequence of turning loose into the anarchic freedoms of the era people raised to obey authority. As a seemingly radical way to return to the conservatism of blind obedience and harsh hierarchy, they were a crevasse between two modes of being into which many people fell.

Sometimes birds return to their cages when the door is open, sometimes people free to make their own choices choose to abandon that power. For a flickering moment in the plaza, I felt vividly, viscerally, what they were offering and why it was alluring to people my age: the possibility of handing back all the weight of responsibility that comes with adulthood, of not having to make decisions every day or deal with the consequences of those decisions, the possibility of returning to something like childhood and arriving at a semblance of certainty that was not hard-won but handed over. I could feel the freedom from agency buried in that surrender of freedom, but I loved my independence and privacy and agency and even some of my deep solitude, and there was never a chance that I was going to give them up.

I've met people who came from happy families who seemed to have little work to do as adults: they would carry on as they had been taught; they were the acorns that didn't fall far from the tree; they were on a road that didn't fork or they had no journey at all ahead, because they had arrived before they set out. When I was young, I envied them the comfort of their certainties. When I was older, I felt the opposite way about lives not requiring so much self-invention and inquiry. There was real freedom to being on my own and a certain kind of peace to being accountable to no one.

I meet young people now who seem clear about their needs and selves, their emotions and others' feelings, in ways that seem astonishingly advanced to me. I too was a wayfaring stranger in that country of inner life, and my attempts to orient myself and find a language to describe what was going on within would be slow, stumbling, and painful. If I had luck in all this, it was the luck of being able to continue to evolve, of being someone gradually, imperceptibly changing, sometimes by intention, sometimes by increments and impulses invisible to me. Of being an acorn that kept rolling. In that little apartment I found a home in which to metamorphose, a place to stay while I changed and made a place in the world beyond. I accrued skills and knowledge and eventually friends and a sense of belonging. Or rather I grew to find that the margins could be the richest place, the perch between realms you could enter and exit.

It's not just that you're an adolescent at the end of your teens, but that adulthood, a category into which we put everyone who is not a child, is a constantly changing condition; it's as though we didn't note that the long shadows at sunrise and the dew of morning are different than the flat, clear light of noon when we call it all daytime. You change, if you're lucky, strengthen yourself and your purpose over time; at best you are gaining orientation and clarity, in which something that might be ripeness and calm is filling in where the naïveté and urgency of youth are seeping away. As I get older now, even people in their twenties seem like children to me, not in ignorance, but in a kind of newness, a quality of discovering many things for the first time, and of having most of their life ahead of them, and most of all of being engaged in the heroic task of becoming.

Sometimes now I envy those people who are at the beginning of the long road of the lives they'll make, who still have so many decisions ahead as the road forks and forks again. Imagining their trajectories, I picture a real road, branching and branching, and I can feel it, shadowy, forested, full of the anxiety and the excitement of choosing, of starting off without quite knowing where you will end up.

I have no regrets about the roads I took, but a little nostalgia for that period when most of the route is ahead, for that stage in which you might become many things that is so much the promise of youth, now that I have chosen and chosen again and again and am far down one road and far past many others. Possibility means that you might be many things that you are not yet, and it is intoxicating when it's not terrifying. Most of the forks in the road I'd confront rose up before me when I lived in that luminous home that Mr. Young made possible for me.

Foghorn and Gospel

The New Strangers Home Baptist Church was two blocks east of my apartment, in a three-story Victorian building with two cross-topped turrets like grain silos on either side of the building and a rare thing in that neighborhood of buildings that came right up to the sidewalk: a small lawn out front, and in the middle of the lawn along with some struggling roses a wooden sign announcing its name. Year after year I passed it contemplating what a new stranger might be. The Solid Rock Baptist Church, up where Lyon Street got steep, was one of several places of worship I'd sometimes pause outside to listen to the gospel music being sung inside. I was an outsider in that neighborhood, a new stranger, even if it was because it was a neighborhood of outsiders to the white society within which I was free to travel and belong.

It was a little neighborhood, five blocks wide, six blocks long, defined by broad boulevards to the east and west, the verdant panhandle of Golden Gate Park to the south, and a steep hill that functioned as a kind of wall to the north. My new home was on the south corner of a block on whose north side was the dim, low-slung Pentecostal church that was also my polling place. Next to it was the liquor store owned by the African immigrant family whose teenage son's funeral I went to many years later, after he was gunned down in a drive-by shooting. The funeral was at the Emanuel Church of God in Christ on Hayes, three blocks away from the family store, less than that from the laundromat in front of which the boy was murdered.

The church was in a pretty building that had once in a paler era been a Mormon church, and the funeral service was rousing, musical, some of the finest oratory I've ever heard. The neat, angular little stucco church painted in pastels always looked like it had fallen out of one of the quattrocento paintings of the lives of the saints. Across from it was the little storefront church I once, in my first years there, attended; the crucifix above the altar was made of egg cartons, bumpy side out. There were several more black churches in that small area. You were never very far from devotion.

A beautiful mansion painted pure white hosted the Brahma Kumaris Meditation Center, and when AIDS became a worldwide scourge later in the decade, Mother Teresa's Missionaries of Charity opened an AIDS hospice in a big wooden Victorian house across the street from my home, and the nuns in thin white cotton saris with blue borders became a regular sight in the neighborhood. Mother Teresa made a few appearances herself, and the nuns once showed me a photograph of her with our Arab-owned, black-run liquor store behind her. There was an Islamic center to the east, a Jesuit university to the west, Catholic and Episcopalian churches on the northern edge, and, to the southeast, just beyond the neighborhood's boundaries, on Divisadero Street, the St. John Coltrane

African Orthodox Church with its jazz masses, food programs, and big Russian Orthodox–style paintings of black archangels.

Which is to say that it was a deeply, densely spiritual neighborhood, a small place shouting to the heavens and to various versions of God. In those first years, the people who attended those little churches walked to them, clad in splendor, the men and boys in suits of many colors, the girls and women in dresses, the older women often in hats in satin, tulle, and velvet that had been folded, clustered, tilted, piled, veiled, decorated with fabric flowers or feathers or jewels. The neighborhood was alive in a way that made the suburban places I'd grown up in seem dead and bereft, those subdivisions that were by design and ethos about withdrawal from public space and human contact, where the adults drove and people kept to themselves, and the fences between houses were taller than our heads.

Sometimes I would look down from my bay windows at churchgoers strolling in various directions, sometimes I would stroll through the throngs of people greeting one another before and after service. It was a vitally alive place in those days when the congregations moved through each other toward their places of worship and dispersed back into their homes on foot. The churches owned their buildings and stayed put, but their members were mostly renters and gradually more and more of them lived somewhere else, and the streets were no longer so lively. Instead of celebratory bustle on the sidewalks, there were lines of double-parked cars near each of them. Then, slowly, the houses of worship also began to vanish, but that was long after those days I was first getting to know the place and its people.

The older residents had been part of the great migration of

black people from the South, and their way of living in the neighborhood seemed to have as much to do with the South and small towns and rural life as with inner city vitalities. Hearing their stories I felt the ghosts of these other places present as origins and memories and templates in this place. San Francisco's black population had increased almost tenfold in the 1940s, and the newcomers had concentrated in this neighborhood close to the city's geographical center, and in Hunter's Point, in the far southeast of the city, where the shipyard jobs were.

These elders were not in a hurry; they were country people. They kept an eye on passersby, greeting the people they knew, sometimes calling out to a child who seemed out of line to them. It was they who taught me that a conversation even between strangers could be a gift and a sport of sorts, a chance for warmth, banter, blessings, humor, that spoken words could be a little fire at which you warmed yourself. Many years later when I spent time in New Orleans and other parts of the South, they felt oddly like home to me, and I realized that this bit of the West Coast had been an outpost of the black South in those days.

2

Mr. Young himself had grown up in rural Oklahoma, and Mr. Ernest P. Teal, who lived across the street but kept a long, luxurious 1970s car in one of the garages in our building, had come from Texas. Mr. Teal was always dressed elegantly, in some variation on a sport coat and a fedora, often with tweed and texture. He was a stylish man who told me stories about the Fillmore District's jazzy heyday, but also a devout man of great and radiant kindness and graciousness, living proof that cool and warmth could emanate from the same source.

Around the corner was Mrs. Veobie Moss, who had inherited the house from her sister, who had bought it with savings made by working as a domestic. When she grew old and forgetful she often sat on her wooden front steps facing south, and when I'd stop to chat, she'd tell me about growing up on a fruit farm in Georgia and how beautiful the fruit trees were. It was as though on those steps she was sitting in two times and places, as though in each conversation she summoned her lost world until we were both in the shade of her beloved orchards. Sometimes I imagined all these old people asleep in the homes around me dreaming of the places they came from, imagined the phantoms of those fields and orchards, dirt roads and flat horizons, shimmering in our middle-of-the-night streets.

Mr. Young was a World War II veteran, and it was the war that had plucked him out of the countryside and brought him here. His military records say he was an unmarried farmworker when he was drafted in Choctaw County, Oklahoma, at age twenty-two. He had stayed in the military, served long enough to get a pension. He told me he had been one of the black soldiers on whom poisonous gas was tested. He described a warehouse or hangar full of gas and men without gas masks running across it. Some of them died, he said.

He drove a big brown pickup truck with a camper shell and kept it parked in the garage just to the left of the building's entryway. He often stood in the garage doorway, leaning against the jamb or the truck, greeting passersby, carrying on conversations, throwing out a word to keep a kid in line; in summer he often hauled a load of melons from Vallejo to sell. Sometimes I caught a glimpse of a pistol tucked into the side of the overalls. He smoked a pipe filled with sweet tobacco whose smell sometimes came upstairs through the vents in my kitchen, which was just above his bedroom. I always stopped to have a conversation when I ran into him, or at least an exchange of pleasantries, and sometimes when I was in a rush I dreaded meeting him in the hall, because anything under five minutes of conversation seemed to be regarded as rude.

He told me stories about growing up in southeastern Oklahoma, the son of sharecroppers. The one I remembered best was about when he was a youth just entering his teens and the Barrow Gang—Bonnie and Clyde and their associates—were in the house when he and his parents came back from the fields. The gang of bank robbers was there because in a segregated society the last place you would look for white outlaws was among black people. The gang reportedly did this with at least one other black share-cropper family in Oklahoma, and I later heard that another legendary gangster, Pretty Boy Floyd, also hid out among black homes in that time when the bank robbers were folk heroes of a sort. On that visit to the Youngs' family home, they left a ten-dollar gold piece on the table or the dresser. His mother didn't want to take stolen money, but his father said, "The children need shoes for winter." There were two visits. That time or another time they came home from the fields and the gang was at their table, helping themselves to food.

So many years after I heard the story, I still see the picture that formed as I listened, of a wooden house somewhere in the country, a table, a sideboard, maybe a porch, maybe surrounded by cornfields. Maybe one of the powerful cars the Barrow gang stole pulled up alongside it, white people in a black family's space. Which is what I was in that building he'd invited me into, in that neighborhood to which many black residents had moved as they were evicted by the gutting of the Fillmore District in the name of urban renewal, nicknamed Negro removal back then, the same families who had come to escape the South pushed out again, pushed to the western margin of a vast area known as the Western Addition.

There are so many ways people are forced to disappear, uprooted, erased, told that this is not their story and not their place. They pile up in layers like geological strata; Ohlone people had resided for millennia on the San Francisco peninsula before the Spanish came crashing in, and Spain claimed the whole coast and then it became a sparsely inhabited outer edge of an independent Mexico. After California and the Southwest were taken by the United States, the Mexicans resident there were fleeced of their vast ranchos and treated as an underclass, as intruders, or both, though their names stayed on many places, the names of saints and ranchers.

Just north and west of our neighborhood lay the immense nineteenth-century cemetery district from which the dead were evicted by the tens of thousands in the early to mid-twentieth century, so that the land could be put to more profitable use. Their skeletons were piled up in mass graves a few cities to the south, their tombstones used as building material and landfill, and a park just south of us had gutters lined with shattered tombstones, some with inscriptions still legible. A short walk east was Japantown, a community from which, during the war, nearly everyone of Japanese descent was forced into internment camps, their vacated homes soon occupied by the black workers and families migrating to where the shipyard and other wartime jobs were. All of that lay in the neighborhood's past when I arrived, though knowledge of it lay far ahead of me.

I had first visited the building and met Mr. Young five days after Ronald Reagan's inauguration. The nation, having reached its maximum of economic equality, had voted in someone who was going to reverse direction, stop black progress, reconcentrate wealth in the hands of the few, dismantle the programs that had helped so many rise, create mass homelessness. Crack was soon to come to the city and other cities, and to our neighborhood and our block. My own experiences around that time with the sense of potency and grand destiny cocaine produced made me wonder whether it was seductive specifically as a counter to the despair and desolation this reversal brought, the drug you took when you hit the wall built to keep you out. There were other walls, prison walls behind which some of the men in the neighborhood would go, and graves for yet others. The Western Addition was black, but realtors and others carved out spaces in part by renaming them, chipping away at the place's identity, as the black community was pushed out of an increasingly expensive, elite city. (Later on I'd come to understand gentrification and the role that I likely played as a pale face making the neighborhood more palatable to other pale faces with more resources, but I had no sense at the start that things would change and how that worked.)

The beautiful wooden houses had been built in the late nineteenth and early twentieth centuries with all the era's lavish ornamentation: bay windows, pillars, lathed railings, ornamental moldings, often with botanical motifs, fish-scale shingles, porches framed in arches, turrets, even the occasional onion dome. They were full of biomorphic curves and eccentric intricacies that made them seem organic, as though they had grown rather than been built. A Muir Woods park ranger once remarked to me that she saw in these structures the great redwood forests that had been cut down to build them, and so those tall groves up and down the coast were another ghostly presence.

The materials and craftsmanship of the original buildings were magnificent, but by the postwar era white flight was taking one population to the suburbs and letting other populations— nonwhite, immigrant, poor—into these places that were treated like slums by their absentee owners. The buildings had their ornamentation scraped off and stucco or plastic siding pasted over their wood, or they were divided up into smaller apartments, often built with shoddy materials and techniques, and many of them were allowed to grow shabby and rickety.

Blight was the code word used in the 1950s and 1960s to justify knocking down many of them to the east of our little neighborhood, leaving behind open wounds in the city's skin of structures. In some of them, grim housing projects were built, some so alienating and oppressive that they were torn down a few decades after they were erected. Other lots in the heart of the Fillmore, which had once been the vibrant cultural zone Mr. Teal liked to reminisce about, were still sitting vacant through most of the 1980s, behind cyclone fencing. A place had been killed, and it never quite came back to life.

Change is the measure of time, my photographer friend Mark Klett likes to say, and little things shifted. When I had arrived, there was a Kodak photo booth on the corner a block west, back when film was how you got photographs, and a glass-walled phone booth on the corner across from my place, next to the liquor store. It became a pay phone bolted to the wooden wall, under a hood like a stove hood, and then disappeared altogether as mobile phones proliferated.

The texture of that bygone life seems hard to convey now: the solitude of a wanderer in the city who could wait for a bus or a taxi to come by or find a phone booth to call a taxi or a friend from a memorized number or by asking the operator or by looking it up in the ruffled tissue-thin pages of the phone book if there was one there, dangling in its black case from the metal cord; who'd look for what she wanted in many stores before the internet meant that you could pinpoint things without getting out of bed, back when there were fewer chain stores and more variety. We were subject to the wonders and frustrations of unpredictability and better able to withstand them because time moved at what would only later seem a gentle flow, like a river across a prairie before the waterfall of acceleration we would all tumble over. We were prepared for encounters with strangers in ways that the digital age would buffer a lot of us from later. It was an era of both more unpredictable contact and more profound solitude.

In that less expensive era, eccentricity had many footholds. A lot of small businesses doubled as museums devoted to various things—there was a dry cleaner near the Castro with a display of antique irons artfully arranged, and various stores with ancient photographs of the neighborhood as it had been long ago, and a corner store in the Mission with a rubber-band ball several feet in diameter, sitting on the linoleum near the chips. The Postcard Palace in North Beach sold nothing but old postcards, most already stamped and inscribed in the confident penmanship of their era with cryptic or jaunty messages from long-dead people to other long-dead people. I still have dozens I bought, a few at a time, mostly black and white, of various mountain roads and chapels and grottoes, on evenings when I wandered out of a punk show to browse there.

The city felt like something old and crumpled with dust and treasures caught in its crevices, and then it was smoothed out and swept clean and some of its people were pushed out as though they had themselves been dirt. A junk shop became a high-end pizzeria, a storefront church became a hair salon, a radical bookstore became an eyeglass boutique, and a lot of things became sushi bars. The place became blander, with more chain stores and more cars, and without flyers layered atop each other on telephone poles, without family pharmacies and odd businesses like old temples where the priest still performed the rites whether or not the congregation had moved on.

There was an actual lunch counter at the Scully Owl Drug Store a couple of blocks to the west of my apartment, like the lunch counters of the South that people sat in at to protest segregation, and then the lunch counter vanished, and then the drugstore was gone, and then, at the millennium, the whole place with the union grocery store, liquor store, butcher, and bakery was bulldozed to build a big chain supermarket with condominiums on top. Many cities that had been centers of blue-collar labor and the manufacture of tangible goods saw these industries die in the postwar era, but their death was not much noticed when new information and finance and tourism metropolises were exploding into being in their ruins, as was the case, spectacularly, in San Francisco by the 1980s. In that era, Silicon Valley was actually manufacturing silicon chips in clean rooms staffed by immigrant workers and dumping the toxins, and then those jobs went overseas and the tech industry began to supernova, and a region that had been an idyllic edge and sometimes an exception became a powerful global center.

Change is the measure of time, and I discovered that in order to see change you had to be slower than it, and that by living in one place for a quarter century, it became visible to me. Gradually. Not at first. People came and went in the building I stayed in, and many of the transient inhabitants imagined that they were passing through a stable neighborhood, but they were part of what was changing it, a river of people scouring out the place, making it less and less black, more and more middle class. The newcomers lived in the space their money secured, not the space that belonged to everyone, and a vitality faded away as the neighborhood became less a neighborhood.

3

My own building, a stucco structure from the 1920s among all those more stately wooden Victorians, had its own graces and charms. My little apartment amused me for the devices built into it as though it was tiny when it felt so spacious: a narrow ironing board that folded into the wall, a Murphy bed that dominated the room when it was opened up, so I unfolded it for good inside what had been a roomy closet. There was a window at the head of the bed, a wide door at the side, and another at the foot of the bed, so it was fairly open as closets go, but still a closet, the one I slept in for a quarter century.

Poverty is sometimes a great preserver of the past, and I lived in a place little altered since its creation. The narrow planks of the yellow-gold oak floors were original, as were the steamy radiator, and the chute on the back stairs through which garbage plummeted two stories into the big can, and the early, tiny, defunct refrigerator built into the wall on one side of the kitchen, by the sinks, across from the built-in sideboard and glass cabinets that rose to the ceiling.

A magnificent old Wedgewood stove presided over the kitchen, creamy white enamel with black trim and a black stovepipe making a right angle on its way to the wall. The pilot lights were never relit while I was there, so I collected matchbooks from bars and restaurants, back when smoking was permitted in those places. Being able to cook meals, to have a whole refrigerator, felt luxurious after the residential hotel in which I'd been unable to store and prepare food.

I was poor. I scrounged furniture off the street and clothes from thrift stores and housewares from rummage sales; we valued old things then, and aesthetically this method suited me. Most of what I owned was older than me, and I relished that; every object was an anchor to the past. I craved a sense of time, history, mortality, depth, texture that had been absent from my upbringing in a newly built suburban edge of the Bay Area with parents whose immigrant urban backgrounds left them with little sense of lineage, few stories, no heirlooms. My work as a writer was sometimes going to be about restoring lost and forgotten pasts to Western places.

I found a small velvet-and-nailhead Victorian sofa at a rummage sale on my way to a demonstration in the Castro District; the gay men selling it for $10 kindly hauled it over and up the stairs after the protest was over. It left droppings of ancient horsehair stuffing on the floor like an incontinent old pet. I accumulated small souvenirs, treasures, and artifacts that made the place gradually come to resemble an eccentric natural history museum, with curious lichen-covered twigs and branches, birds' nests and shards of eggs, antlers, stones, bones, dead roses, a small jar of yellow sulfur butterflies from a mass migration in eastern Nevada, and, from my younger brother, a stag's antlered skull that still presides over my home.

I was passing through poverty and I would gradually return to financial ease; in poverty too I was a new stranger but I spent enough years there to grasp a little of how it works and what it does. In another sense poverty as a poverty of the spirit had been all around me since birth. My parents had ingested a deep sense of lack during the Great Depression or out of whatever deprivations their childhoods contained, and they were not interested in sharing their middle-class comfort. I did not trust that they would have bailed me out if something truly horrific had prostrated me, and I was never willing to fall apart enough to find out, so I was not slumming quite the way that a lot of young white people around me were, who could opt out of poverty as easily as they had opted into it. I left it too, but slowly, by my own labors. And as I'd understand better later, by the advantages that had come with my color and my background that made me feel fit, to myself and in the eyes of others, for an education and white-collar work.

I read books standing up in bookstores or got them from libraries or searched for months or years to find the cheapest used copy; I listened to music on the radio and made cassette tapes of albums at friends' houses; I eyed things and was spurred and pricked and bothered by the promise things make, that this pair of boots or that shirt will make you who you need or want to be, that what is incomplete in you is a hole that can be stuffed with stuff, that the things you have are eclipsed by the things you want, that wanting can be cured by having, beyond having what is essential.

I always wanted something more, something else, and if I got it I wanted the next thing, and there was always something to want. Craving gnawed at me. I wanted things so badly, with a desire that was so sharp it gouged me, and the process of wanting often took up far more time and imaginative space than the actual person, place, or thing, or the imaginary thing possessed more power than the real one. And then once I had something the craving died down—it was the craving that was so alive—and then that craving appeared again, gaping and reaching after the next thing. Of course with lovers and boyfriends, uncertainty could keep craving alive (and with the more reliable and kinder men, that metamorphosed into that other kind of attachment we call love).

More than anything I wanted transformation not of my nature but of my condition. I didn't have much of a vision of where I wanted to go, but I knew I wanted to distance myself from where I had come from. Perhaps that was not so much a matter of craving as its opposite, aversion and escape, and perhaps it was why walking was so important to me: it felt like I was getting somewhere.

I did have one early vision of what a life worth living could look like. When I read her diaries in my mid-teens, Anaïs Nin's evocations of her Parisian life between the wars gave me images of spaces that could harbor conversational depths and exploration, of lives that intertwined and cross-pollinated, of the warmth of being wrapped up in passionate friendships. Many years later, after a dinner party of friends gathered around the chrome-legged linoleum table in my kitchen, the radical historian Roxanne Dunbar-Ortiz, one of the guests, and I agreed that this was what we had hungered for in our lonely youths. (And many years later I was dismayed to find out that Nin had left her banker husband out of the published diaries, so she presented herself as more hand-to-mouth bohemian than she really was.)

Next to the stove were two wide sinks, one an ordinary kitchen sink, the other, to the right, a deep laundry sink I covered over with the old enameled metal dish-drainer tray that had come with the place, and the dank dark deep sink under the tray would grow fetid, so that I had to lift the lid off and scour it out from time to time. Women had washed clothes by hand in it, and in the first years I was there, the building's flat roof still had a wooden cage for hanging out laundry to dry, up the last flight of stairs whose upper steps crunched with gravel from the tarry roof.

The kitchen's original yellow-and-green linoleum flooring was worn into something grainy and cracked that was impossible to keep clean, so I painted it black, and then painted it again and again as it wore out again and again. But the light streamed into the kitchen every sunny morning, and into the other room's east-facing bay window and trickled through the south bay window all day in winter. That last window faced Fulton Street and a streetlight, and sometimes I would sit there transfixed watching the fog cascade over itself like gargantuan, phantasmagorical tumbleweeds under the streetlight, as the wind pushed it in from the cold ocean where it had arisen.

Or I'd lie in bed and hear in the hush of night the foghorns blaring far away. Awakening in the middle of the night, in the center of a city and a place thought of as the inner city, I often heard the foghorns, and they carried me to the edges and beyond, to the sea, the sky, and the fog. I heard them often, and in recollection the sound seems almost like a correlative of that middle-of-the-night state of being not quite awake, not quite asleep, with a wandering mind but a body pinned down by sleep's Jupiterian gravity. They called to me as though I was a lost ship, not to bring me home but to remind me of the ocean and the air beyond and that there in the closet I was still connected to them.

I lived there so long the little apartment and I grew into each other. In the beginning I had hardly anything in it, and it felt vast, and at the end it was overstuffed with books and with many boxes of papers under the bed, and it felt cramped. In memory it seems as lustrous as a chambered nautilus's mother-of-pearl shell, as though I was a hermit crab who had crawled into a particularly glamorous shelter, until, as hermit crabs do, I outgrew it.

A dozen years since I've left it I can still see every detail, still imagine sometimes that I'm reaching for the medicine cabinet there rather than the one I actually live with, still gave the Lyon Street address to a taxi driver automatically when I went back to walk its streets again before I recollected that I had not lived there in many years, and recited the next address after that and finally the current one that will never be tattooed on my psyche the way that place was. When I lived there, I often dreamed of the street that ran past my childhood home, turned into a country road, and then ended in a horse pasture, the road from which I slipped through barbed-wire fences to so many of my adventures, but now I dream of that little apartment on Lyon Street as a foundational place the way I dreamed of the road then.

When it was still my home, I dreamed many times about finding another room in it, another door. In some way it was me and I was it, and so these discoveries were, of course, other parts of myself. I dreamed over and over of my childhood home as a place I was trapped in, but this place wasn't penning me in but opening up possibilities to me. In dreams it was bigger, it had more rooms, it had fireplaces, hidden chambers, beauties that didn't exist in waking life, and once the back door opened onto radiant fields instead of the drab clutter that was really there.

The kitchen walls had once been covered in vinyl brick-patterned wallpaper whose seams showed through the white paint on the back wall behind the stove, so one day I pulled it off. It was like tearing bandages off a wound. It came off in great sheets, pulling the surface of the next layer of wallpaper off as it came. Underneath was the inner layer of an older, more beautiful wallpaper, patterned with lattices of ivy. When I saw the pale brown pattern, I felt the vivid presence of the people who had lived there before me, more ghosts, other times, from before the war, when the neighborhood was another kind of place with other kinds of people on another kind of earth.

Then I dreamed about doing the same thing, and in the dream version I revealed a dense collage of newspaper and magazine pages and scraps of fabric, a lot of floral images, all in rosy hues, luscious and strange, a garden of scraps. In the dream I knew it was a souvenir of another woman who'd been there before me, an old black woman with a gift for making.

The building was located near the center of the city, and thinking of it now I see it as the axis on which a compass needle swings, a place that opened to the four directions. I didn't make a home there; it made me, as I watched and sometimes joined communities, wandered thousands of miles on foot in the city over the years, sometimes over familiar routes to the movie theaters or to bookstores or groceries or work, sometimes for discovery as I climbed the hills, and sometimes for respite from the density and turmoil when I went to Ocean Beach to be reminded that this was the place where a lot of stories reached their end and, across the vast Pacific, others began.

The churning ocean and the long sandy beach were another kind of home and another kind of refuge, in the vastness that put my woes and angst in proportion to the sky, the sea, the far horizon, the wild birds flying by. The apartment was my refuge, my incubator, my shell, my anchor, my starting blocks, and a gift from a stranger.

Life During Wartime

A friend gave me a desk not long after I moved into the apartment, a woman's small writing desk or vanity, the one I am writing on now. It's a dainty Victorian piece of furniture, with four narrow drawers, two on each side and a broader central drawer above the bay in which the sitter's legs go, and various kinds of ornamentation—doweled legs, each with a knob like a knee, knobby ornaments, scallops on the bottom of the drawers, drawer pulls like tassels or teardrops.

There are two pairs of legs on the front, two on the back, set beneath the side drawers. Despite all the frills, the old desk is fundamentally sturdy, an eight-legged beast of burden whose back has carried many things over the decades, or two beasts of burden side by side, yoked together by the desktop. The desk has moved with me three times. It's the surface on which I've written millions of words: more than twenty books, reviews, essays, love letters, several thousand emails to my friend Tina during the years of our near-daily epistolary exchange, a few hundred thousand other emails, some eulogies and obituaries, including those of both of my parents, a desk at which I did the homework of a student and then a teacher, a portal onto the world and my platform for reaching out and for diving inward.

A year or so before she gave me the desk, my friend was stabbed fifteen times by an ex-boyfriend to punish her for leaving him. She almost bled to death; she had emergency transfusions; she was left with long scars all over her body, which I saw then without response because whatever capacity to feel had been muffled, maybe when I got habituated to violence at home, maybe because it was something we were supposed to take in stride and be nonchalant about, back when few of us had language to talk about such violence or an audience ready to listen.

She survived; she was blamed for what happened as victims often were then; there were no legal consequences for the would-be murderer; she moved far from where it happened; she worked for a single mother who was evicted, and who gave her the desk in lieu of wages; and then she gave it to me. She moved on and we lost touch for many years, and then reestablished it, and she told me the full story, a story that could make your heart catch fire and the world freeze over.

Someone tried to silence her. Then she gave me a platform for my voice. Now I wonder if everything I have ever written is a counterweight to that attempt to reduce a young woman to nothing. All of it has literally arisen from that foundation that is the desktop.

Sitting at that desk to write this, I went to the online photography archive of the city that my public library maintains, hoping to recall a little of what the old neighborhood looked like. The fourth photograph for the street I lived on was from June 18, 1958, of a house a block and a half away, and it bore this caption: "Curious passersby peer down an alley, alongside 438 Lyon Street, where the body of Dana Lewis, 22, nude except for a black bra, was found today. Police, after a preliminary examination, said bruises on the victim's throat indicated that she might have been garroted by a length of rope." It's clear her death is a spectacle for the newspaper as well, which describes her in titillating terms, while the passersby are described as curious rather than distressed by the sight of a corpse.

She was also known as Connie Sublette, and it turns out her death got a lot of attention in the papers at the time. Mostly, the accounts blamed her for it, because she was a sexually active young bohemian who drank. SEAMAN DESCRIBES CASUAL SLAYING, said one headline, with the tag PLAYGIRL VICTIM. SLAYING CLOSES SORDID LIFE OF PLAYGIRL said another, in which *sordid* seems to mean that she had sex, adventures, and sorrows, and *playgirl* means she deserved it. Her age is given as twenty or twenty-four. Dana Lewis or Connie Sublette's ex-husband was said to have lived at 426 Lyon, where she went seeking comfort with him after her boyfriend, a musician, fell to his death at a party.

Al Sublette wasn't home or didn't answer, so she wept on his front steps until the landlord told her to go away. A sailor, by his own account, offered to get her a taxi and killed her instead. The newspapers seem to have taken his word that the killing was an accident and that while devastated by loss she had agreed to have sex with him in an alley. BEATNIK GIRL SLAIN BY SAILOR LOOKING FOR LOVE said one headline, as though strangling someone to death was an ordinary part of looking for love. "She had stars in her eyes and wanted to go all the time," said her ex-husband. Allen

Ginsberg, who had taken photographs of Al but not of Connie Sublette, noted her death without comment in a letter to Jack Kerouac on June 26, 1958. She was known, but hardly mourned.

I didn't know what had happened at 438 Lyon Street, but I did know that the poet and memoirist Maya Angelou had lived not far to the northeast during her adolescence, not long after the end of the five years of muteness that was her response to being raped repeatedly at age eight. And I knew about the apartment a few blocks in the other direction from my own, at 1827 Golden Gate Avenue, into which nineteen-year-old newspaper heiress Patty Hearst was brought in a thirty-gallon garbage can after her kidnapping by the Symbionese Liberation Army, a small delusional would-be revolutionary group, in early 1974. She was, she testified, kept blindfolded and bound for weeks in a closet in this location and a previous one and raped by two of her kidnappers. These two stories found their way into the news. But most never did or they were small items on the back pages.

Some I witnessed. Once late at night, out the window of my apartment, I saw a man with a huge knife in one hand cornering a woman in the doorway of the liquor store across the street. When a police car drifted up silently and the officers surprised the knife wielder, he slid the weapon away along the sidewalk and claimed as its steel clattered on concrete, "It's okay. She's my girlfriend."

The writer Bill deBuys began a book with the sentence "A species of hope resides in the possibility of seeing one thing, one phenomenon or essence, so clearly and fully that the light of its understanding illuminates the rest of life." And then he begins with the pine desk at which he's writing and travels from a description of the grain and color of the wood to trees and forests and keeps going into love, loss, epiphanies of place. It's a lovely journey. I can imagine many forests into which I'd rather go from my own desk, which was made of trees that must have been cut down before my grandmothers were born, than into the violence against my gender.

But the desk I sit at is a desk given to me by a woman who a man tried to murder, and it seems time to tell what it meant to me to grow up in a society in which many preferred people like me to be dead or silent and how I got a voice and how it eventually came time to use that voice—that voice that was most articulate when I was alone at the desk speaking through my fingers, silently—to try to tell the stories that had gone untold.

Memoirs at their most conventional are stories of overcoming, arcs of eventual triumph, personal problems to be taken care of by personal evolution and resolve. That a lot of men wanted and still want to harm women, especially young women, that a lot of people relished that harm, and a lot more dismissed it, impacted me in profoundly personal ways but the cure for it wasn't personal. There was no adjustment I could make in my psyche or my life that would make this problem acceptable or nonexistent, and there was nowhere to go to leave it behind.

The problems were embedded in the society and maybe the world in which I found myself, and the work to survive it was also work to understand it and eventually work to transform it for everyone, not for myself alone. There were, however, ways of breaking the silence that was part of the affliction, and that was rebellion, and a coming to life, and a coming into power to tell stories, my own and others'. A forest of stories rather than trees and the writing a charting of some paths through it.

2

It felt ubiquitous then. It still does. You could be harmed a little—by insults and threats that reminded you you were not safe and free and endowed with certain inalienable rights—or more by a rape, or more by a rape-kidnapping-torture-imprisonment-mutilation, more yet by murder, and the possibility of death always hung over the other aggressions. You could be erased a little so that there was less of you, less confidence, less freedom, or your rights could be eroded, your body invaded so that it was less and less yours, you could be rubbed out altogether, and none of those possibilities seemed particularly remote. All the worst things that happened to other women because they were women could happen to you because you were a woman. Even if you weren't killed, something in you was, your sense of freedom, equality, confidence.

My friend Heather Smith remarked to me recently that young women are urged to "never stop picturing their murder." From childhood onward, we were instructed to not do things—not go here, not work there, not go out at this hour or talk to those people or wear this dress or drink this drink or partake of adventure, independence, solitude; refraining was the only form of safety offered from the slaughter. During those years at the end of my teens and the beginning of my twenties, I was constantly sexually harassed on the street and sometimes elsewhere, though *harassed* doesn't convey the menace that was often present.

The former Marine David J. Morris, author of a book on posttraumatic stress disorder, notes that the disorder is far more common and far more rarely addressed among rape survivors than combat veterans. He wrote me, "The science on the subject is pretty clear: according to the *New England Journal of Medicine*, rape is about four times more likely to result in diagnosable PTSD than combat. Think about that for a moment—being raped is four times more psychologically disturbing than going off to a war and being shot at and blown up. And because there are currently no enduring cultural narratives that allow women to look upon their survival as somehow heroic or honorable, the potential for enduring damage is even greater."

In war the people who try to kill you are usually on the other side. In femicide, they're husbands, boyfriends, friends, friends of friends, guys on the street, guys at work, guys at the party or in the dorm, and, the week I write this, the guy who called a Lyft and stabbed the pregnant driver to death and the guy who went into a bank and shot five women and the guy who shot the young woman who took him in when his parents kicked him out, to name a few examples of the carnage that made it into the news. Morris calls PTSD "living at the whim of your worst memories." But he also suggests that war, as an atmosphere in which you live in fear of attack, mangling, annihilation, and in which people around you suffer those afflictions, can traumatize you even if you are physically untouched, and the fears can follow you long after what gave rise to them. Mostly when people write about the trauma of gender violence, it's described as one awful, exceptional event or relationship, as though you suddenly fell into the water, but what if you're swimming through it your whole life, and there is no dry land in sight?

Legions of women were being killed in movies, in songs, in novels, and in the world, and each death was a little wound, a little weight, a little message that it could have been me. I once encountered a Buddhist saint who had worn tokens devotees gave him; they loaded him up, tiny token by tiny token until he was dragging hundreds of pounds of clinking griefs. We wore those horror stories as a secret weight, a set of shackles, that dragged along everywhere we went. Their clanging forever said, "It could have been you." During this time, I gave away the only television I ever owned, my maternal grandmother's little black-and-white model from her nursing home, not long after an evening when I turned the dial and found that a young woman was being murdered on each channel. It could have been me.

I felt hemmed in, hunted. Over and over, women and girls were attacked not for what they'd done but because they were at hand when a man wished to—to *punish* is the word that comes to mind, though for what might linger as a question. Not for who but for what they were. We were. But really for who he was, a man who had the desire and believed he had the right to harm women. To demonstrate that his power was as boundless as her powerlessness. In the arts, the torture and death of a beautiful woman or a young woman or both was forever being portrayed as erotic, exciting, satisfying, so despite the insistence by politicians and news media that the violent crimes were the acts of outliers, the desire was enshrined in the films of Alfred Hitchcock, Brian De Palma, David Lynch, Quentin

Tarantino, Lars von Trier, in so many horror movies, so many other films and novels and then video games and graphic novels where a murder in lurid detail or a dead female body was a standard plot device and an aesthetic object. Her annihilation was his realization. For the intended audience, it was apparently erotic, because in life women kept getting murdered in the course of sex crimes, and the fear of assault, of rape, was also a fear of violent death.

Which was a reminder that I was, we were, not the intended audience for so much art, including the stuff lauded as master-pieces and upheld as canonical. Sometimes the male protagonists protected women, particularly beautiful young white women, from other men, and protector was one face of their power, but destroyer was still the other face, and either one put your fate in their hands. They protected what was theirs to protect or destroy, and some-times the plot was about his grief that he'd failed to protect, or his revenge against other men, and sometimes he destroyed her him-self, and the story was still about him.*

She was dead even before she was a corpse; she was a surface, a satellite, an accessory. In comics, the violent death of a woman as a plot device in a story focused on a man was so common that women coined a term for it, *fridging*, after the 1999 website Women in Re-frigerators documenting the plethora of gruesome endings for fe-male characters. In the video gaming world, young women who criticized the misogyny in video games were for years harassed

---

*That men on the margins should be punished for sexual violence, especially against white women, and that privileged and powerful men should not reinforces a hierarchy of relative value. It's one in which what is being protected is not women per se, but who has property rights over which women (as was explicit in earlier laws that treated rape as trespass or damage of another man's property and, into the 1980s in the USA, that reserved a hus-band's right to rape his wife, and almost never punished white men for raping women of color).

with doxing and death and rape threats. Some, after grisly and detailed threats of harm, had to leave their homes and take extraordinary security precautions; that is, they had to disappear. Protecting women from online surveillance, threats, and harassment became an avocation for feminist cybersecurity experts.

As I write, there are new TV serials about the horrific torture-murder-dismemberment of women. One flirts around the periphery of the torture-death of twenty-two-year-old Elizabeth Short in Los Angeles in 1947 that was given the unduly elegant name "Black Dahlia murder"; the other is about the 1970s serial torturer, rapist, and murderer Ted Bundy, played by a handsome young star. It's far from the first movie about Bundy, and the L.A. murder of Short has begotten a small publishing industry unto itself. When Givenchy came out with a Dahlia Noir perfume, advertised with the slogan "the fatal flower," I wondered if it meant that women should aspire to smell like a mutilated corpse. But even the old ballads were full of rapes and murders and grievous bodily harm, as were pop songs from Johnny Cash to the Rolling Stones to Eminem.

Feminists of an earlier era insisted that rape is about power, not erotic pleasure, though there are men for whom their own power or a woman's powerlessness is the most erotic thing imaginable. For some women too, so we learn that our helplessness and peril is erotic, and accept or reject or struggle with the sense of self and stories that come with them. Jacqueline Rose wrote in 2018, "Sexual harassment is the great male performative, the act through which a man aims to convince his target not only that he is the one with the power—which is true—but also that his power and his sexuality are one and the same thing."

Though each incident I experienced was treated as somehow isolated and deviant, there were countless incidents, and they were of the status quo, not against or outside it. Talking about it made people uncomfortable, and mostly they responded by telling me what I was doing wrong. Some men told me they wished someone would sexually harass them, because they seemed to be unable to imagine it as anything but pleasant invitations from attractive people. No one was offering the help of recognizing what I was experiencing, or agreeing that I had the right to be safe and free.

It was a kind of collective gaslighting. To live in a war that no one around me would acknowledge as a war—I am tempted to say that it made me crazy, but women are so often accused of being crazy, as a way of undermining their capacity to bear witness and the reality of what they testify to. Besides, in these cases, crazy is often a euphemism for unbearable suffering. So it didn't make me crazy; it made me unbearably anxious, preoccupied, indignant, and exhausted.

I was faced with either surrendering my freedom in advance or risking losing it in the worst ways imaginable. One thing that makes people crazy is being told that the experiences they have did not actually happen, that the circumstances that hem them in are imaginary, that the problems are all in their head, and that if they are distressed it is a sign of their failure, when success would be to shut up or to cease to know what they know. Out of this unbearable predicament come the rebels who choose failure and risk and the prisoners who choose compliance.

There was a feminist movement in full swing in the 1980s, with much to say about violence against women, even the Take Back the Night marches against it, but it was not within reach for me at the time. I was too young, too immersed in cultures out of keeping with that culture of what seemed like mostly older women, and they spoke a language I hadn't yet learned. They were at a distance I would slowly traverse, after all this violence would make a solitary feminist of me. I wrote about violence against women in a cover story for a punk magazine in 1985, in art criticism and essays in the 1990s, in a chapter of my history of walking in 2000 detailing all the obstacles women face in walking out in the world.

There's a kind of indignation I know well, when someone feels that the wrong done them has been unrecognized, and a kind of trauma that makes the sufferer into a compulsive storyteller of an unresolved story. You'll tell it until someone lifts the curse by hearing and believing you. I've been that person with firsthand experiences sometimes, but something of that was what I felt about violence against women in general.

Back then when it was so personal, I was told to move to someplace more affluent (though some of my most malevolent harassment occurred in such places), to get a car, to spend money I didn't have on taxis, to cut my hair, dress as a man or attach myself to a man, to never go anywhere alone, get a gun, learn martial arts, to adapt to this reality, which was treated as something as natural or inevitable as the weather. But it wasn't weather; it wasn't nature; it wasn't inevitable and immutable. It was culture, it was particular people and a system that gave them latitude, looked the other way, eroticized, excused, ignored, dismissed, and trivialized. Changing that culture and those conditions seemed to be the only adequate response. It still does.

It could have been me who found herself in a moment in which my fate was not my own, my body was not my own, my life was not my own, and I hovered on that brink and was haunted by it for a few years that reshaped my psyche in ways that will never be over. Which was, perhaps, the point: to remind me that I would never be entirely free. This violence mostly targets girls and young women as an initiation rite, a reminder that even after you cease to be a frequent target you're vulnerable. Each death of a woman was a message to women in general, and in those days I was tuned in to survival with a kind of dread and shock at finding out that I lived in an undeclared war. I wanted it declared, and I have to the best of my ability declared it myself from time to time.

It was popular in the media and polite conversation to pretend that murderers and rapists were marginal men, them and not us, but during that time a white man who was a bank vice president strangled a teenage sex worker in my suburban hometown not quite thirty miles north of San Francisco while his wife and daughters were at Girl Scout camp. It was the era of the Night Stalker and the middle-aged white man known as the Trailside Killer (who raped and killed women hikers on the trails I hiked on) and the Pillowcase Rapist and the Beauty Queen Killer and the Green River Killer and the Ski Mask Rapist and many other men who rampaged up and down the Pacific Coast without nicknames.

Two or three years before this narrative begins, a fifteen-year-old runaway had been kidnapped near San Francisco, raped, and had her forearms chopped off by her rapist, who assumed she'd bleed to death in the culvert he dumped her in. She lived to testify and went on to make an ordinary life for herself. He murdered another woman when he got out of prison. Her story haunted me and the friend who'd given me the desk. I found it again in Shakespeare's *Titus Andronicus*, where Lavinia is raped and has her hands cut off and her tongue cut out to silence her but manages anyway to convey who ravaged her. And again in Greek mythology, when, after he rapes her, Philomela's brother-in-law cuts out her tongue to silence her.

I've heard and read many accounts by women who were impacted by a single brutal attack, but the horror for me lay in the pervasiveness of this violence. I had a sense of dread in those days, a sense that the imminent future of my body might be excruciating and horrifying. There was a mouth of rage that wanted to devour me into nothing, and it might open up almost anywhere on earth.

3

I had never been safe, but I think some of the horror that hit me was because for a few years I had thought that maybe I could be, that male violence had been contained in the home I grew up in, and so I could leave it behind. I wrote once that I grew up in an inside-out world where everywhere but the house was safe, and everyplace else had seemed safe enough as a child in a subdivision on the edge of the country, where I roamed freely into town or into the hills that were both right out the door. I'd yearned to leave home and planned to do so since I was a child in single digits making lists of what to take to run away. Once I left home I was almost never in danger inside my home again, but by then home often felt like the only place I was safe.

At twelve and thirteen and fourteen and fifteen, I had been pursued and pressured for sex by adult men on the edge of my familial and social circles, and I'd been the target of street harassment in other places. There are absences so profound that even knowledge of their absence is absent; there are things missing even from our lists of the missing. So it was with the voice with which I could have said *No, I'm not interested, leave me alone*, I realized only recently.

We often say silenced, which presumes someone attempted to speak. In my case, it wasn't a silencing because no speech was stopped; it never started, or it had been stopped so far back I don't remember how it happened. It never occurred to me to speak to the men who pressured me then, because it didn't occur to me that I had the authority to assert myself thus or that they had any obligation or inclination to respect my assertions, or that my words would do anything but make things worse.

I became expert at fading and slipping and sneaking away, backing off, squirming out of tight situations, dodging unwanted hugs and kisses and hands, at taking up less and less space on the bus as yet another man spread into my seat, at gradually disengaging, or suddenly absenting myself. At the art of nonexistence, since existence was so perilous. It was a strategy hard to unlearn on those occasions when I wanted to approach someone directly. How do you walk right up to someone with an open heart and open arms amid decades of survival-by-evasion? All this menace made it difficult to stop and trust long enough to connect, but it made it difficult to keep moving too, and it seemed sometimes as though it was all meant to wall me up alone at home like a person prematurely in her coffin.

Walking was my freedom, my joy, my affordable transportation, my method of learning to understand places, my way of being in the world, my way of thinking through my life and my writing, my way of orienting myself. That it might be too unsafe to do was something I wasn't willing to accept, though everyone else seemed more than willing to accept it on my behalf. Be a prisoner, they urged cheerfully; accept your immobility, wall yourself up like an anchorite! I was driven to go somewhere that was partly a metaphysical urge to make a life, to become and transform, to do, but literal travel expressed that passion and let off that pressure; I was never going to give up walking. It was a means of thinking, of discovering, of being myself, and to give it up would have meant giving up all those things.

One day when I was walking past a small park just east of the neighborhood, a passerby I'd never seen before spat full in my face without stopping. Even with other people around, I was alone: I was harassed more than once on the bus home while everyone pretended nothing was happening, perhaps because a man in a rage intimidated them too, perhaps because in those days people more often considered it none of their business or blamed the woman. Men would make proposals, demands, endeavor to strike up conversations and the endeavors quickly turned into fury. I knew of no way to say No, I'm not interested, that would not be inflammatory, and so there was nothing to say. There was no work words could do for me, and so I had no words.

Usually I'd look down, say nothing, avoid eye contact, do my best to be as absent, unobtrusive, insignificant as possible—invisible as well as inaudible—since I was afraid of that escalation. Even my eyes had to learn deferential limits. I erased myself as much as possible, because to be was to be a target. Those men conducted a conversation, sometimes a shouting match, with my silence. They shouted I owed them words, obedience, deference, sexual services. But the time I told off a man—a well-dressed white man—who was following me, in the same kind of profanity-laced language he was using to me, he was genuinely shocked and then threatened to kill me. It was daytime in a tourist district, so he probably wasn't going to try, but it was a frightening reminder of what speaking up achieved.

It was as though their desire was overtaken by resentment or fury that the desire would not be satisfied, that the overtures would be rebuffed, and since they knew that in advance, the desire and rage emerged together in obscene, scornful propositions, in language that demonstrated their right to say those things and my helplessness to not suffer the insults. The rage: it was as though they expected me to obey strangers, as though any woman belonged to any man, as though everyone, anyone, owned me except me. The words: they had an overabundance, and I had none, even though I lived for and by words the rest of the time.

Even when I spoke to others, my words seemed useless. Late one night, a huge man whose muscles swelled his tracksuit followed me off a bus—not my usual bus line, but one that at that hour ran more frequently through another neighborhood and left me farther from home—and shadowed me on my several-block walk. Nearly home, I saw a uniformed security guard and asked him for help, thinking that after all this was his job. He turned more slowly than I did—and as he did, I saw the man following me step behind a fence—and said I was imagining things, and left. The stalker reappeared. I made it home.

Another night, after another late-night ride on the same bus line, I was mugged on the same street—surrounded by tall young men, one of whom pinned my arms down while I shouted at passing cars that did not stop, and while I imagined that all my worst fears were about to come to pass. I lost a whole satchel full of negatives and prints for a photojournalism class along with other schoolwork. The photography professor did not seem to believe me, and my grade suffered from the makeup work that was not as good as the work that was stolen. I was training to be a journalist, but my capacity to report was doubted. My words failed again. And again. After another attack, I told my boss—an elderly child psychiatrist—about it because I needed to explain why I wasn't doing my job well that day, until I realized he was erotically excited by the attack. My friend who was almost murdered had faced the same kind of response from the men around her afterward.

I was often told that I was imagining things, or exaggerating, that I was not believable, and this lack of credibility, this distrust of my capacity to represent myself and interpret the world, was part of the erosion of the space in which I could exist and of my confidence in myself and the possibility that there was a place for me in the world and that I had something to say that might be heeded. When no one else seems to trust you, it's hard to trust yourself, and if you do, you pit yourself against them all; either of those options can make you feel crazy and get called crazy. Not everyone has the backbone for it. When your body is not your own and the truth is not your own, what is?

I was twenty-one or twenty-two when I went to a New Year's Eve party at the home of gay friends in suburban Marin County, the county of the Trailside Killer and that homicidal banker. My boyfriend at the time was running the lights for a concert, but was supposed to come and join me at midnight. He was delayed by his diligence, and I was sad that we were not celebrating the New Year together. I didn't have a car in those days, I didn't want to ask anyone for a ride, so I set out well after midnight to walk to my mother's house about a mile away, where I could slip in and sleep on the couch without disturbing anyone. Perhaps she was away; that part I don't remember, but what came before was indelible.

While I was on the main thoroughfare between the two houses, I realized that someone was behind me. I turned around: it was a big man with a shaggy beard and long hair. I walked faster. He was only a couple of feet behind me, not at a normal distance, and we were the only two people out on foot at that hour. It was dark, and the shrubs dividing the dark homes from each other loomed and streamed shadows, and his shadow and mine swelled and shrank from streetlight to streetlight, and cars passed by and their headlights made all the shadows swirl and lurch.

Once I had spotted him he began to speak, a low, steady stream telling me that he wasn't following me, that I should not trust my own judgment, an accelerated course of gaslighting designed to undermine my ability to assess the situation and make decisions. He was very good at what he did, and his insinuating sentences were disorienting to the very young woman I was. Clearly, he had a lot of practice. I wondered later what harm he had done to other women before and after.

So much of what makes young women good targets is self-doubt and self-effacement. Now I would flag down cars, stand in the middle of the road, make noise, bang on doors, respect my own assessment of the threat, and take any action that seemed likely to get me out of it. I would bother someone, anyone. But I was young and trained not to make a fuss and to let others determine what was acceptable and even to determine what was real. It was many years later that I stopped letting men tell me what had and had not happened.

On that dark boulevard, I behaved as though it wasn't happening, though I crossed the street to see if he was following me. He stuck to me like a curse. The walk seemed endless, though I was hoping to get to my destination before he attacked, thinking that if I didn't disrupt the stalemate perhaps neither would he. Cars passed. Shadows swirled. I crossed the street again. He followed. Again. Again. Finally a few blocks before my destination, a man in a sedan pulled up and leaned over to open the passenger door and offered me a ride.

The stalker murmured from very close behind, "Don't you know that getting into a stranger's car is the most dangerous thing you can do?" Of course I had been told that over and over, and I hesitated.

Then I got in.

The driver said, "I passed you once and thought that it was none of my business. Then I thought it looked like a Hitchcock movie, so I came back."

I'm grateful a man rescued me from a man. I wish I had not been in a Hitchcock movie where I needed rescue.

Though I was followed and yelled at and mugged and grabbed and more than once strangers threatened to kill me and men I knew menaced me a few times and others pursued me uncomfortably long after I'd tried to discourage them, I was not raped, though many friends of mine were, and all of us spent our youths navigating the threat, as do most women in most places. It gets you even if it doesn't get you. All those years, I noticed the little stories tucked away on newspaper back pages, given a paragraph or two, mentioned in passing on broadcasts, about dismembered sex workers and murdered children and tortured young women and long-term captives, about wives and children slain by husbands and fathers, and the rest, each one treated as an isolated incident or at least something that was not part of any pattern worth naming. I connected the dots, saw an epidemic, talked and wrote about the patterns I saw, waited three decades for it to become a public conversation.

The threat of violence takes up residence in your mind. The fear and tension inhabit your body. Assailants make you think about them; they've invaded your thoughts. Even if none of these terrible things happen to you, the possibility they might and the constant reminders have an impact. I suspect some women push it down to some corner of their mind, make choices to minimize the reality of the danger so that it becomes an unseen subtraction of who they are and what they can do. Unspoken, unspeakable.

I knew what was lost. And the weight of it crushed me then, in those years when I was starting out, when I was trying to make a life, have a voice, find a place in the world. I did all those things, but I joked later that not getting raped was the most avid hobby of my youth. It took considerable vigilance and wariness and constantly prompted changed routes through cities, suburbs, wild places, through social groups, conversations, and relationships.

You can drip one drop of blood into a glass of clear water and it will still appear to be clear water, or two drops or six, but at some point it will not be clear, not be water. How much of this enters your consciousness before your consciousness is changed? What does it do to all the women who have a drop or a teaspoon or a river of blood in their thoughts? What if it's one drop every day? What if you're just waiting for clear water to turn red? What does it do to see people like you tortured? What vitality and tranquility or capacity to think about other things, let alone do them, is lost, and what would it feel like to have them back?

At the worst point, I would sleep with the lights and the radio on so it would seem as though I was still alert. (Mr. Young told me men had come by and asked which apartment I lived in, which of course he didn't tell them, but it fed my nervousness.) I didn't sleep well and still don't. I was, as they say of traumatized people, hypervigilant and I was setting up my home to appear hypervigilant too. My flesh had turned to something brittle with tension. I used to look at the thick steel cables holding up the Golden Gate Bridge and think of the muscles in my neck and shoulders that felt as taut and as hard. I startled easily and flinched—cringed, really—when anyone made a sudden movement near me.

I tell all this not because I think my story is exceptional, but because it is ordinary; half the earth is paved over with women's fear and pain, or rather with the denial of them, and until the stories that lie underneath see sunlight, this will not change. I tell this to note that we cannot imagine what an earth without this ordinary, ubiquitous damage would look like, but that I suspect it would be dazzlingly alive and that a joyous confidence now rare would be so common, and a weight would be taken off half the population that has made many other things more difficult to impossible.

I tell it too because when I wrote about all these things in general—in the objective voice of editorials and surveys of the scene—I didn't represent enough of the way it harms you, or rather the way it harmed me. There's a passage in Sohaila Abdulali's book on surviving rape about a kind of voice—"a way of telling the story in a smooth arc; matter-of-factly, with intonation but no real emotion. . . . No matter how many details we share, we leave out the unbearable ones that nobody wants to hear." In my book on walking I wrote, "It was the most devastating discovery of my life that I had no real right to life, liberty and pursuit of happiness out of doors, that the world was full of strangers who seemed to hate me and wished to harm me for no reason other than my gender, that sex so readily became violence, and that hardly anyone else considered it a public issue rather than a private problem," but that too didn't quite plunge into what it was like inside my head.

Danger wracked my thoughts. Scenarios of attack would arise unbidden, and sometimes I addressed them by imagining winning the combat, usually by means of martial-arts moves I'm not really capable of, and so I killed in order not to be killed over and over during the grimmest years of that era, in imagined scenarios that were intrusive, unwanted, anxiety-driven, a kind of haunting and a way of trying to take control of being haunted. I realized then that making you think like a predator was one thing predators could do to you. Violence itself had penetrated me.

I had more ethereal ways of coping. Casting about for strategies to be safe, I imagined protective clothing, and if you imagine clothing sufficient to stop harm, you imagine armor, and then, if you were me, you'd end up with the full medieval metalware pile. I became preoccupied with armor for a few years and visited it in museums and read up on it in books, imagined being inside it, aspired to try it on. Toward the end of this time a friend of mine became a studio assistant to a New York artist, Alison Knowles, whose husband, Dick Higgins, was from the wealthy family that had established the Higgins Armor Museum in Worcester, Massachusetts. I wrote him a letter asking if he could arrange for me to try on armor, making the request cheerful, cerebral, an interesting experiment rather than a fantasy born out of agony.

I never got closer to the armor, and it was an imaginative and not a practical solution. What is armor after all but a cage that moves with you? But maybe being in that cage would have freed me in some way. Or maybe I was in it and both freed and stifled by it: when I think of who I was then and often am now, the hard reflective, defensive surface of armor seems like a good image for it. There's a way you can throw all your consciousness into that surface, into being witty, vigilant, prepared for attack, or just so stressed out your muscles lock up and your mind locks down. You can forget your own tender depths and how much of life that matters takes place there beneath the surface and the surfaces. It's still easy to be the armor. We die all the time to avoid being killed.

Images of levitation also arose unbidden as I revisited or imagined attacks; I dreamed often of flying, but I wasn't asking for that full freedom, just imagining lifting out of reach, however many feet that might be above the head of a pursuer. If I could not have a body too solid to be harmed, an armored body, could I have one too ethereal to be part of the clashes on the surface of the earth?

I imagined that so earnestly that I can still feel and see myself rising up to the level of the street lamp outside my apartment, hovering there in the halo of light in the night, safe not just from predators but from the laws of physics and the rules governing human bodies and perhaps from the vulnerability of being a mortal who had a body and lived on earth and from the weight of all those fears and that hate.

Disappearing Acts

1

One night late in my teens, my friend who'd given me the desk and a friend of hers and I walked down Polk Street, the lower stretch of the street where the bright lights of the cheerful old buildings with late-night bars and stores gave way to taller, blanker facades that cast longer shadows and where the runaway children sold themselves to the men who purchase children. We were walking in the dark, and I was reciting the refrain to a song that had taken possession of me, that I couldn't get out of my head, that had a power that seemed as though it could be my power, so perhaps I possessed it instead, like an amulet, a spell I could cast, a fuel that could surge through me and make me something unstoppable.

It was "Mercenaries (Ready for War)" by John Cale, the avant-garde musician and sometime rocker who cofounded the Velvet Underground. I must have heard it on the radio because I never owned the record. The lyrics, if you read them, are full of scorn for soldiers, but the rhythm and the voice said something else.

Disapproval was the railroad tracks but power was the train rumbling over them; the song had it both ways. The force of the thundering drum and bass and the howling, raging man's voice intoning "Ready for war" over and over was a soldier's power, was itself a desire for war, a hypervigilance that was a high, a readiness for anything, an armor made out of attitude. I didn't want a war, but since there was one, or many, I wanted to be ready for it. Or them. "Just another soldier boy" went another of its refrains.

I didn't imagine myself as a man but in those moments when I felt swept up by power that surged like confidence and sureness, I didn't imagine myself as a woman. I wanted to be rugged, invincible, unstoppable, and I didn't have examples of women who were those things. But I lost myself in the moment and the music; to be myself was to be, it seemed then, outside that power or unable to access it, to be vulnerable not in the sense of openhearted, but prone to harm. I think that a lot of girls and young women have this yearning that is part desire to have a man and part desire to be him, to merge with this force, to be where power is, to be powerful, to cleave unto it in the self or by bringing your body to it as an offering and as a quest for transmission. To be the armor and not what's vulnerable behind it.

At fifteen, I had fallen in love with punk rock when it was first appearing on the U.S. scene. It gave form and voice to my own fury and explosive energy, in lyrics about defiance and indignation, in music that thumped and galloped. It was at first, in the late 1970s, music for outsiders and the participants were mostly scrawny, idealistic, experimental. Early slam dancing was people harmlessly bouncing into and off each other. Then the nerds were shoved aside for the jocks as a bunch of burly Southern California men's bands came to dominate what had morphed into hardcore or thrash, and the front of the concert halls and clubs became a gladiatorial arena dominated by strong young men and the occasional woman who would knock you down and trample you if you couldn't hold your own. It came to seem like another place I didn't really belong.

But for a while, it spoke for me and to me and through me, and one day late in my teens I walked down the street chanting that song from John Cale's most punk-influenced album. It was as though I had a choice between being fearless and powerful or being myself and I had no map for where those two things might intersect. They seemed like parallel lines that would run alongside each other forever.

2

here do you stand? Where do you belong? Those are often questions about political stances or values, but sometimes the question is personal: Do you feel like you have ground to stand on? Is your existence justified in your own eyes, enough that you don't have to retreat or attack? Do you have a right to be there, to participate, to take up space in the world, the room, the conversation, the historical record, the decision-making bodies, to have needs, wants, rights? Do you feel obliged to justify or apologize or excuse yourself to others? Do you fear the ground being pulled out from under you, the door slammed in your face? Do you not stake a claim to begin with, because you've already been defeated or expect to be if you show up? Can you state what you want or need without its being regarded, by yourself or those you address, as aggression or imposition?

What does it mean neither to advance, like a soldier waging a war, nor to retreat? What would it be like to feel that you have that right to be there, when *there* is nothing more or less than the space you inhabit? What does it mean to own some space and feel that it's yours all the way down to your deepest reflexes and emotions? What does it mean to not live in wartime, to not have to be ready for war?

Some of it comes from your position in society, and all the usual factors of race, class, gender, sexual orientation, and more that come into play, some from a quality for which *confidence* is too glib a word. Perhaps *conviction* or *faith* is better. Faith in yourself and your rights. Faith in your own versions and truth and in your own responses and needs. Faith that where you stand is your place. Faith that you matter. Those people who have it in full seem rare to me, and clear in a way the rest of us aren't; they know who and where they are, how and when to respond, what they do and don't owe others. Neither retreating nor attacking, they reside in a place that doesn't exist for the rest of us, and it's not where the overconfident who take up too much space and take space away from others reside.

Perhaps I will always live in questions more than answers. What's yours? Where are you welcome, allowed? How much room is there for you; where do you get cut off, on the street or in the profession or the conversation? All our struggles can be imagined as turf battles, to defend or annex territory, and we can understand the differences between us as being, among other things, about how much space we are allowed or denied, to speak, to participate, to roam, to create, to define, to win.

One of the struggles I was engaged in when I was young was about whether the territory of my own body was under my jurisdiction or somebody else's, anybody else's, everybody else's, whether I controlled its borders, whether it would be subject to hostile invasions, whether I was in charge of myself. What is rape but an insistence that the spatial rights of a man, and by implication men, extend to the interior of a woman's body, and that her rights and jurisdiction do not cover even that territory that is herself? Those altercations on the street were about men asserting their sovereignty over me, asserting I was a subject nation. I tried to survive all that by being an unnoticeable nation, a shrinking nation, a stealth nation.

At the same time, I was toiling to appear by becoming a writer, to lay claim to having something to say, to deserve participation in the conversation that was culture, to have a voice, and that meant other contests in other territories. Those came a little after the years when menace on the street wracked me with fear and tension. And I was trying to have a life, including a love life, which meant appearing, attracting, being attracted, and sometimes I enjoyed men, enjoyed my body, my appearance, my time in public. But the war made it all more complicated.

Conversations are another territory where questions arise about who may take up space, who is interrupted or harassed into silence, that condition of occupying no verbal space. At its best, a conversation is a joy and a collaborative construction, building an idea, an insight, sharing experiences; at its worst it's a battle for territory, and most women have experiences of being pushed out one way or another, or not let in in the first place, or being assumed not to be qualified to participate. Eventually that would become one of my subjects.

3

Sometimes having a body seemed to be the problem, having a body that exposed me to danger and potential harm and also to shame and shortcomings and the problems of how to connect and how to fit in, whatever that meant, whatever feeling I imagined people who were confident about their bodies and their movements and their memberships felt. Having a body of my gender was a vulnerability and shame so vast that I still find myself casting about for defenses, for versions of that armor I dreamed of in my twenties.

I was convinced that my body was a failure. It was a tall, thin, white body, which is supposed to be the best thing to be in terms of how the culture as a whole values and rates female bodies. But I saw my own version of this as a catalogue of wrongnesses and failures and confirmed and potential shame. The rules about women's bodies were exacting, and you could always measure your distance from the ideal, even if it was not a great distance. And even if you got over your imperfections of form, the realities of biology, of bodily functions and fluids, were always at odds with the feminine ideal, and a host of products and jokes and sneers reminded you of that. Perhaps it's that a woman exists in a perpetual state of wrongness, and the only way to triumph is to refuse the terms by which this is so.

No one is ever beautiful enough, and everyone is free to judge you. In her memoir *Under My Skin*, Doris Lessing describes how, when she was a young woman at a dance, a middle-aged stranger told her that she had an almost perfect body but one breast was a third of an inch too high or too low—I can't remember which, just that a stranger thought her body was under his jurisdiction and announced what must have been a wholly imaginary fault to demonstrate his right and capacity to render judgment and her subjection to it.

Men were always telling me what to do and be; once in my emaciated youth I was walking through North Beach eating a pastry from one of the Italian bakeries when a portly middle-aged man chastised me for eating it because I should be watching my weight. Men told me to smile, to suck their dicks, and when I owned an old car with loose battery cables, men would wander by to tell me what needed fixing when I threw up the hood to wiggle the battery cables, and the ones who spoke were always wrong and never seemed to notice I already knew what I was doing.

The problem isn't really with bodies, but with the relentless scrutiny to which they're subjected. The problem is being a woman. Or being a woman subject to men. My once-Catholic mother's deep shame about the female body's functions and form had been passed on with vigor, and my father's tendency to criticize her anatomy and then mine and sometimes those of women passing by in the most clinical terms didn't help, nor did it that these were not un-usual but ordinary parts of a culture that obsessed over bodies and in those days quantified female beauty according to precise mea-surements and sizes, and told us that the rewards were boundless for meeting them, the punishments for failing endless, and pun-ished all of us anyway, because these were ultimately standards ev-eryone would fail to meet.

And so there I was where so many young women were, trying to locate ourselves somewhere between being disdained or shut out for being unattractive and being menaced or resented for being at-tractive, to hover between two zones of punishment in space that was itself so thin that perhaps it never existed, trying to find some impossible balance of being desirable to those we desired and being safe from those we did not.

We were trained to please men, and that made it hard to please ourselves. We were trained to make ourselves desirable in ways that made us reject ourselves and our desires. So I fled. My body was a lonely house. I was not always home; I was often elsewhere. I imag-ined when I was young some science-fiction version of humans be-coming brains in jars as a good thing, that our bodies were some sad thing we were mired in rather than instruments of joy, connec-tion, and vitality, the non-negotiable terms of our existence. It's no wonder I was thin, no wonder women were so praised for being thin, for taking up as little room as possible, for hovering on the brink of vanishing, no wonder some of us vanished through under-eating like a country ceding territory, an army retreating, until it ceased to exist.

I had a body. I had been a small, wiry child, withdrawn but active in my own pursuits, roaming the hills and climbing trees, and then at thirteen I suddenly grew several inches, and it took many years for my flesh to catch up with my bones. I was five feet seven and less than a hundred pounds when I left home, and then weight came gradually, slowly, enough to push me over to a hundred that first year I was away from home and by my thirties I was more or less average. But for a long time I was unusually thin, not lean like young women who have little fat over their muscle, because I had so little muscle either.

My skeleton was not far from the surface. My iliac crests jutted out so that people sometimes thought I was carrying something in the front pockets of my jeans. I thought of them as pearl-handled revolvers. When I let the bathwater drain out while I lay in the tub a pool formed on my hollow belly. My ribs showed. I had a waist so small a gay man once quipped that I did not have a torso but, like a wasp or a bee, an abdomen and a thorax. It was my friend David Dashiell, and he used the word *thorax*, and we were friends partly because we could banter like that.

There is a picture taken by the man who was walking with us while I sang "Ready for War" shortly after I moved into the apartment. It's of me in a gray 1940s suit I wore constantly as my dress-up outfit, or rather of me wearing the suit's pencil skirt and a man's vest turned backward and belted into a sort of backless top, without the jacket. I have my back to the camera, I'm pressed up against the wall with its rectangles of molding, head turned to the right, a little hat with a veil over a face that still looks childish, a back that looks vulnerable, unformed, and elbow-length black gloves on. I'm trying to take shelter in my shadow.

The clothing speaks of an attempt to be elegant, sophisticated, to be an adult, to be ready for the world and find a world ready for me, a portrait of all those aspirations of youth. The posture speaks of an attempt to elude and melt away. I'm trying to appear and to disappear at once. The waist of that skirt I measured before I gave it away when I was pretty sure it would never fit again unless I became deathly ill; it was twenty inches.

Being so thin made me frail, tired, limited in my energies, easily chilled; maybe it made me more of a target: I was the opposite of robust, and all that punk rock was partly an attempt to imbibe a spirit that would counter the frailty, or perhaps it was that my flesh was frail but my spirit was savage. I sometimes think I fled to the city in my youth because to run in the other direction, to the country or the wilderness, would have required a physical vigor that I didn't have then. I could walk great distances, I could dance for hours, but I had waves of fatigue that were probably blood-sugar drops when I could hardly stay awake, and I had dizzy spells when I stood up suddenly, and I was often tired.

Being thin is seen as a virtue, as a consequence of discipline, and self-restraint, and so it's often admired as though it is a sign of character. But it's often just a sign of the genetic lottery or that phase of youth before the flesh catches up with the bones. Some people insisted that I was so thin because of anorexia or bulimia, eager to make what they envied pathological, undesirable (and there were years of jokes about concentration camp victims and comparisons of me to famine victims, as though my body was itself a disaster zone).

There's an austerity to thinness, to having a hard body, to being closer to the solidity of bone than the softness of flesh. It's as though you're removed from the messy, squishy, leaky business of life, as though you're looking on from outside, from someplace less mortal, less malleable. As though you disdain mortality and the pleasures of the flesh. It's an irreproachably stern way to show up. Which is to say that thinness is a literal armor against being reproached for being soft, a word that means both yielding, cushiony flesh and the moral weakness that comes from being undisciplined. And from consuming food and taking up space.

Women's bodies are usually soft if they're healthy, at least in some places, and if softness is equated to a moral failing, and virtue to a low-body-fat hardness of surface, then that's another way in which to be a woman is to be wrong, one that people starve their way out of. Roxane Gay wrote in her book *Hunger* that "we should not take up space. We should be seen and not heard, and if we are seen, we should be pleasing to men. . . . And most women know this, that we are supposed to disappear, but it's something that needs to be said, loudly, over and over again, so that we can resist surrendering to what is expected of us."

Maybe starvation is how you apologize for existing, or slip toward nonexistence, but I was not trying to make myself thin. I was already there, and I ate, but food wasn't one of the main things I was hungry for. I was hungry for love, but that was so strange and foreign and terrifying a phenomenon I approached it obliquely and described it with euphemisms and fled from some versions and failed to recognize others. I was hungry for stories, books, music, for power, and for a life that was truly mine, hungry to become, to make myself, to distance myself as far as possible from where I was in my teens, to keep going until I arrived someplace that felt better.

Later in my twenties, an older man I was seeing said, "Baby, you're driven," and in that age when I threw out sharp replies without thinking, I said all too accurately, "And you're parked." I was driven, to redeem my existence by achievement, to keep going until

I reached a better place (and when I did, the habit was too ingrained for me to slow down), to make something, to stop being what I was and become something else, to meet all the demands placed on me, and of course to meet everyone else's needs first or instead. There was real joy in the creative and intellectual life, but also a withdrawal from all the other realms of life. I was like an army that had retreated to its last citadel, which in my case was my mind.

That physical diminution has its equivalents in how we live and move and act and speak or withdraw from doing so. Lacy M. Johnson writes of a relationship so controlling that, when she left him, the man built a padded room in which to rape and murder her and from which she escaped after the former and before the latter: "I tried diminishing myself in such a way that I wouldn't provoke him, wouldn't anger him, tried to bend myself according to his pleasure so that he would like everything I did and said and thought. It didn't matter, because no matter what I did, it was never enough. I kept at it anyway, until there was almost nothing left of me, of the person I had been. And that person I became, who was barely a person of her own, is the version of me he liked best."

Femininity at its most brutally conventional is a perpetual disappearing act, an erasure and a silencing to make more room for men, one in which your existence is considered an aggression and your nonexistence a form of gracious compliance. It's built into the culture in so many ways. Your mother's maiden name is often requested as the answer to a security question by banks and credit card companies, because it's assumed her original name is secret, erased, lost as she took on the name of a husband. It's no longer universal for women to give up their names but still rare to pass them on if they're married, one of the ways women vanish or never appear.

So much was so absent that its absence was rarely noted, the lack built into the current arrangements and the possibility that things could be otherwise. Many lists of the missing have been augmented in my lifetime; we still fail to perceive voices, assumptions, positions that we will recognize in times to come. We often say silenced, which presumes someone attempted to speak, or we say disappeared, which presumes that the person, place, or thing first appeared. But there are so many things that were never murmured, never showed up, were not allowed to enter rather than forced to exit. And there are people who showed up and spoke up who were not seen or heard; they were not silent, not invisible, but their testimony fell on deaf ears, their presence was not noted.

When I was young, human beings were routinely described as mankind, and mankind could be described as a singular man, and he, and even men in liberation movements—Martin Luther King Jr., James Baldwin—fell back on this language, because the absence of women was so absent from our imaginations that few noted that it even could, let alone should, be otherwise. The 1950s brought books like *The Family of Man* and *LIFE's Picture History of Western Man*; the 1960s a conference and book titled *Man the Hunter* that all but wrote women out of evolutionary history; by the 1970s we got a long BBC series about *The Ascent of Man*. The current online edition of the *Oxford English Dictionary* notes, "*Man* was considered until the 20th cent. to include women by implication, though referring primarily to males. It is now frequently understood to exclude women."

This had real consequences. They are endless but a few come to mind: heart attacks were described by how they affected men, so that women's symptoms were less likely to be recognized and treated, a situation from which many women died; crash test dummies replicated male bodies, meaning that vehicular safety design favored male survival, and women died at higher rates. The Stanford Prison Experiment of 1971 presumed that the behavior of young men at an elite university could be universalized to stand for that of all humanity, and William Golding's 1954 novel *Lord of the Flies*, about a group of younger British schoolboys, was also often cited as an example of how humans behave. If men were everyone, then women were no one.

When I was young, nearly everyone who held power and made news was male, and pro sports, TV sports, meant men's sports, and many newspapers had a women's section about domesticity and style and shopping that implied that everything else—the news section, the sports pages, the business section—were men's sections. Public life was for men, and women were consigned to private life, and wife beating was described as a private business though it was legally a crime and crimes were the public's business and the law's. Andrea Dworkin, whose radical feminism was shaped in part by an early marriage to a murderously violent man, said, "I remember the pure and consuming madness of being invisible and unreal, and every blow making me more invisible and more unreal, as the worst desperation I have ever known."

It is so normal for places to be named after men (mostly white men) and not women that I didn't notice it until, in 2015, I made a map renaming places after women and realized I'd grown up in a country where almost everything named after a person—mountains, rivers, towns, bridges, buildings, states, parks—was named after a man, and nearly all the statues were of men. Women were allegorical figures—liberty and justice—but not actual people. A landscape full of places named after women and statues of women might have encouraged me and other girls in profound ways. The names of women were absent, and these absences were absent from our imaginations. It was no wonder we were supposed to be so slender as to shade into nonexistence.

4

I carried other weight. I had and still sometimes have a sense of dread that held down my sense of hope and possibility, a sinking feeling that was a real sensation of heaviness in the chest, as though my heart were encased in lead, as though I were on some planet whose gravity made every step a struggle and the lifting of limbs an onerous exercise and going out among other people an exhausting prospect.

It was a feeling in the present that arose from a vision of a future that was no future, one with no way forward, from a conviction that what is terrible will always be terrible, that *now* is a flat, featureless plain that goes on forever, with no forests relieving it, no mountains rising from it, no doorways inviting you out of it—the dread that nothing will change that somehow coexists with the dread that something terrible is going to happen, that what is joyous cannot be trusted, and what is feared is lying in wait for you. If there's a gravity to this feeling, there's also a geography, that low place in the earth that we call a depression. It seemed to be made out of logic and a real assessment of the situation, but it was weather, and it would disperse like clouds, and gather again like clouds.

If later on I wrote about hope, it was to pass along the ladders of logic and narratives with which I got myself out of these low places I know well.

I had since childhood imagined interrogations in which lacking the right answers was punished, sometimes unto death, interrogations that must have gotten something of their format from quiz shows seen in early childhood as well as the mockery that comes or came with getting something wrong in school or at the dinner table. I set myself exams and races and tests—if I saw a blue car before the bus came, if a bird flew by before I arrived, if I reached the middle of the crosswalk before the first person in the crowd on the other side of the street—like variations on the children's game of "step on a crack/break your mother's back." I set a lot of imaginary parameters that would determine unrelated outcomes; it was an anxious reflex, a distraction, perhaps sometimes a reassurance when the bird flew by, when I got to the far side of the bridge before I let out my breath.

In quiz shows, people are mostly rewarded for knowing obscure things or picking the right thing, but also those who fail are cast into some outer darkness of exile. For this to become a nightmare you just have to imagine that, say, the arbitrary, heavy-handed punitiveness of your parents, or the mockery of your peers, or the violence in the news is attached to these scurries after information that puts you in the safe and rewarding spot of being right.

This seemed, in my mind, to have something to do with Chinese emperors, perhaps from accounts of the old Chinese civil service exams that required extensive memorization. I suppose one of the reasons I squirreled away information was anxiety about this infernal inquisition and the possibility that if you knew the names of the pieces of armor, that if you knew the etymologies of words, the cast of the Wars of the Roses, the routes of pilgrimages, that if you knew which swans are mute and which are black and that *eohippus* means the dawn horse that is the diminutive ancestor of modern horses—a useless amulet of information I've carried around without using since I was a child—that knowledge could protect you from a punitive, incoherent universe.

Perhaps it can, in another way, not by warding off your enemies but by leading to the recognition of patterns and meanings and friends who share your eclectic interests or by making friends of your curiosity and what it finds. After all, Aladdin opens a cave with the right word. And sometimes ideas and sentences and facts are your friends in themselves.

I read, I daydreamed, I wandered the city so ardently in part because it was a means of wandering in my thoughts, and my thoughts were runaways, constantly taking me away in the midst of the conversation, the meal, the class, the work, the play, the dance, the party. They were a place I wanted to be, thinking, musing, analyzing, imagining, hoping, tracing connections, integrating new ideas, but they grabbed me and ran with me from the situations at hand over and over. I disappeared in the middle of conversations, sometimes because I was bored but just as often because someone said something so interesting that my mind chased after the idea they offered and lost track of the rest of what they said. I lived in a long reverie for years, went days without much interruption to it, which was one of the gifts of solitude.

I dreamed of flying over and over. In one dream in 1987 I fled a violent man on railroad tracks and then remembered that I could metamorphose and became an owl with a moth's dusty wings. When the man lunged for me and grabbed my feet, I flew low over the water to drag him through it in the hopes of shaking him off. But mostly they weren't violent dreams, just dreams of being alone, above it all, in the stratosphere, lonely and free. Perhaps being free of the weight of depression and expectation. Of the weight of a body. Of the weight of animosity.

The beauty of those places I soared over is with me still, and in all my dreams as in my waking life was a love of place, a sense that places were embodiments of emotions, were anchors, were companions of a sort, even protectors or parents. Once at the Pacific, I thought to myself *Everything is my mother but my mother*, and I recognized how the ocean had been a mother offering power, constancy, and solace. Many years later when I began rowing a scull, I realized that out in the water, I was out of reach of men and dogs, and that, as well as the beauties of water, made it serene, dreamy, the eighteen-foot span of my oars being as close to having wings as I could come.

But long before that, I flew. Even in the dreams my logical mind wrestled with how this was possible, anxious that it be possible. In one dream I had learned to align myself with the earth's magnetic fields, in another I drew my strategy from a sentence I had read describing how the great dancer Nijinsky seemed to hover in the air a split second longer than gravity made possible, and I too was airborne for that kind of interval in a theater. I was in a world where levitation was normal but I tried to exceed the bounds and go higher. I tasted the cold of the upper stratosphere. Or I streamed across green landscapes.

Sometimes I flew to prove that I could. I was the girlfriend of the poet John Keats and I demonstrated I could fly among blackberry bushes whose fruit the size of street lamps suggested I was, we were, the size of songbirds. Other times I flew across the rooftops of the city and the view was dazzling, as was the sense of having all that space under you, like the sense of all that water when you swim in clear lakes. It was the beautiful spacious side of loneliness.

I wondered what this flying meant. Sometimes it seemed to be dreams' impatience, a jump cut from here to there without filling in the space between. Sometimes it was escape. Sometimes it was a talent, and like talents sometimes do, it set me apart, usually literally, since I tended to fly alone, to be the only one who could fly, though sometimes I showed other people how to do it or carried them along.

It was an experience of not belonging to the ordinary world and not being bound to it. I thought sometimes that it might be about writing, about being a writer, and now I wonder why I didn't think of it as reading, as that constant, chronic activity that had taken up so much of my waking hours since I'd learned to read, as being in a book, in a story, in the lives of others and invented worlds and not my own, unbounded by my own body and my own life and my own time and place.

I could fly, though now I wonder if the problem was how to come to earth.

Freely at Night

One day in 2011, I got a Facebook friend request from someone I'd been in college with when I was seventeen and stayed in touch with for a few years after, someone I cherished then as a person I could trust and talk to, perhaps because of who he was or because of who I imagined he was, or how I filled up what I didn't know about him with what I needed. I accepted the request with enthusiasm and curiosity about what the years we'd been out of touch had brought and who he might be. He replied that my political views were abhorrent, but that he would like to send me copies of the letters I'd written him. Once I found out he was conservative, things that had seemed mysterious or exotic about him when he was young suddenly made sense. I didn't find out more about him, but I did find out from him more about me.

A manila envelope came through the mail slot a few weeks later. I had a little queasiness about meeting that teenager directly, and so I waited several years to open it. In the photocopies of letters written on lined yellow legal pads in a small neat handwriting that is no longer mine I met a person who didn't know how to speak. By that I mean several things. The young writer I met there didn't know how to speak from the heart, though I could be affectionate. But also, she was a jumble of quotations and allusions and foreign phrases and circumlocutions, of archness and pretense and avoidance and confusion, an attempt to use language that kept her so busy that hardly anything got said, or major events were mentioned in passing in sentences busy doing other things that didn't matter. She had collected a lot of words, phrases, syntaxes, tones and was trying them out, like someone at the very first stages of playing an instrument, with squawks and clangs. She was speaking in various voices because she didn't yet know what voice was hers, or rather she had not yet made one.

There was one startling passage in all the verbiage. I'd written about the eighteenth-birthday party I'd thrown my younger brother not quite a year after I'd moved into the apartment. A lot of chocolate frosting had been smeared around on a lot of people, and there was talcum powder on the stereo and towels soaked with champagne in the tub, I mentioned proudly. And then the letter went on to list essays I was trying to write, though it would be a couple of years before I published anything.

I mentioned a "long essay to work it out for myself—about my penchant for long solitary walks at night, the danger involved (I've given it up. I was nearly assaulted a few weeks ago) and how it affects my attitude toward feminism—of what value are the advances made in the last decades when one's physical freedom has become so severely jeopardized. Most urban women, you know, live as though in a war zone. . . . There's a price to pay either way—a year and a half of living dangerously has warped my mind. This essay is going to be a mammoth prose poem, an analysis of (or at least a hymn to) the nature of the night itself."

That essay was never quite written, though I often afterward wrote in praise of darkness, sometimes trying to reverse the metaphors in which good is light or white and black and darkness are evil, with their problematic racial overtones, and I eventually wrote a book called *Hope in the Dark*. Years after this letter, my time in the desert taught me to love shade, shadows, and night as a reprieve from the burning heat and light of day. And four years after that ambitious proposition to write about gender and night, I wrote for the first time about violence against women and the ways that thwarted and limited our access to public space and freedom of movement and equality in any and all arenas and then I wrote about it again and again.

When I wrote my book on walking almost twenty years later, I quoted Sylvia Plath, who declared when she was nineteen, "Being born a woman is my awful tragedy. Yes, my consuming desire to mingle with road crews, sailors and soldiers, barroom regulars—to be part of a scene, anonymous, listening, recording—all is spoiled by the fact that I am a girl, a female always in danger of assault and battery. My consuming interest in men and their lives is often misconstrued as a desire to seduce them, or as an invitation to intimacy. Yes, God, I want to talk to everybody I can as deeply as I can. I want to be able to sleep in an open field, to travel west, to walk freely at night." Reading the passage long after I'd put it in the book, I wondered about who she might have been if she'd had the freedom of the city, as they used to call it, and of the hills, and of the night, of how her suicide in her kitchen at thirty must have been in part from the confinement of women in domestic spaces and definitions.

Children are diurnal animals. Nocturnal life to a newcomer to adulthood was almost synonymous with the new world of sensuality and sexuality, of freedom of movement and exploration, with a lingering sense that the rules fade a little when the sun goes down. Nightlife. Nightclubs. Nightmares. Patti Smith's first hit, "Because the Night," had come out only a few years earlier, telling us that the night belongs to lovers and to love. Love is made mostly in dimness or darkness, and darkness—the failure of sight, the most rational of the senses, the awakening of the other senses, the otherworldliness that the world takes on when it turns away from the sun and faces out into the galaxy—can itself be an erotic embrace.

My bohemian aunt had given me a copy of Djuna Barnes's *Nightwood* when I was eighteen, and I had fallen in love with what that brief novel did with words and with its romantic extravagance about pain and loss. It's mostly remembered as a lesbian novel now, and the love of Nora Flood for the elusive Robin Vote forms the bones of its plot set mostly in Paris. But the ode-like monologues by the garrulous cross-dressing garret-dwelling doctor Matthew O'Connor, "an Irishman from the Barbary Coast (Pacific Street, San Francisco) whose interest in gynaecology had driven him half around the world," dominate it. He is an expert on the night, on night as the mysteries of the human heart and the fluidity of who we are and the foolishness of who we think we are and what we think we should have and hold. "Every day is thought upon and calculated, but the night is not premeditated," he tells Flood. "The Bible lies the one way but the night-gown the other. The night, 'Beware of that dark door!'"

He's an oracle akin to the transgender Tiresias in *Oedipus Rex*, someone who understands men and women and the things they want and imagine and do together and alone. Night is the space in which poetic intuition, not logic, prevails, in which you feel what you cannot see, and perhaps in some sense he is the night itself, or its oracle and high priestess. In that letter to that old friend of my late teens, I was saying that I wanted to bring Barnes's ferocious lyricism to my own immediate experience, to wed the poetics of what I wanted and the politics of why I had trouble reaching it. To whom does the night belong? It did not seem to belong to me.

At least books belonged to me. Closed, a book is a rectangle, thin as a letter or thick and solid like a box or a brick. Open, it is two arcs of paper that, seen from the top or bottom when the book is wide open, look like the wide V of birds in flight. I think about that and then about women who turn into birds and then about Philomela, who in the Greek myth is turned into a nightingale after she is raped, as her brother-in-law pursues her to murder her.

The word *nightingale* is an old one in the English language, cobbled together from *night* and *singer*. I wonder if Keats had Philomela in mind when he wrote his "Ode to a Nightingale," or if I did when I dreamed of him and flying. In it the poet imagines flying himself "on the viewless wings of poesy," into a dark forest—"for here there is no light . . . and tender is the night," a line I was happy to recognize again in F. Scott Fitzgerald's novel, which is also about incest and rape and their unspeakability and the way the harm spreads outward. Both Keats's poetry and *Tender Is the Night* came to me the year I was seventeen and was finally taught some ways to read more deeply, to see a story as made up of layers, echoes, references, and metaphors.

I had read Ovid's *The Metamorphoses*, with the story of Philomela and all those other goddesses, nymphs, and mortals being ravaged, much earlier. In the myths, women keep turning into other things, because being a woman is too difficult, too dangerous. Daphne is turned into a laurel as she flees Apollo; I'd known that even before I'd memorized Andrew Marvell's "The Garden," including these lines:

> *The gods, that mortal beauty chase,*
> *Still in a tree did end their race.*

I'd learned it in the same introductory class where we read Yeats's "Leda and the Swan," which I can see now is creepily specific about the details of a god in the form of a bird raping a woman. "How can those terrified vague fingers push / The feathered glory from her loosening thighs?" That so many Greek myths are about rape and women trying to escape it never came up. It's not that I think we were too fragile to be exposed to this stuff that was everywhere, in pop songs as well as sonnets and classics, just that the fact that the reality, the ubiquity, and the impact of rape were weirdly unspeakable, in art and in life. Our tongues had been cut out too.

Ovid tells us that tongueless Philomela weaves the story of her violation into a tapestry and by signs conveys that the tapestry should be delivered to her sister, the wife of her rapist. When the truth is unspeakable you say it indirectly; when your speech is taken away other things speak; sometimes the body itself speaks with the tics, eruptions, numbness, paralysis that are cyphers for what happened. In the myth, there's more gore, and then the sisters are both turned into birds—and in some versions it's the sister who becomes the night singer, the nightingale. In *A Midsummer Night's Dream*, the fairies call on Philomela when they sing their queen to sleep, evoking maybe the beauty of her singing voice or the ways she's tricked and deceived as a woman.

Keats's nightingale is not the mortal victim but the transcendent figure, impervious to human suffering: "Though wast not born for death, immortal bird," he apostrophizes her. "No hungry generations tread thee down," and I memorized those lines when I first met the poem, or maybe they just stuck, as so many lines I read then have, as though I was laying down a foundation of those bricks. He thinks of her song heard long ago, of the words that last innumerable lifetimes. She is poetry itself or something that poetry—that the durable wings of words and the ether of narrative they generate—brings us to, a sanctuary and a place out of time. A refuge. A place beyond bodies and the flesh. In Philomela's case, the mutation into a nightingale doesn't come in time to save her from rape, mutilation, silencing, and imprisonment, but it does save her from murder, if being turned into something other than yourself is survival.

A book: a bird that is also a brick. I arranged my battered paperback library on stacks of plastic milk crates I pilfered one at a time from in front of the liquor stores when they were closed, and then returned them to where they'd come from when I managed to acquire some wooden bookshelves. My birds flocked, and eventually a long row of shelves narrowed the hallway and half filled the main room and piled into unstable pillars on my desk and other surfaces.

You furnish your mind with readings in somewhat the way you furnish a house with books, or rather the physical books enter your memory and become part of the equipment of your imagination. I was building up a body of literature, points of reference for a map of the world, a set of tools to understand that world and myself in it by reading. Mostly I wandered in books on my own, or read what was given me, an indiscriminate omnivore then, as the young often are with people as well: not sure what their criteria are, what feeds them and what discourages them. So I read what came my way and then learned enough to trace paths through the forests of books, learn landmarks and lineages.

I loved the physical objects that are books too and still do. The codex, the box that is a bird, the door into a world, still seems magical to me, and I still walk into a bookstore or a library convinced that I might be on the threshold that will open up onto what I most need or desire, and sometimes that doorway appears. When it does, there are epiphanies and raptures in seeing the world in new ways, in finding patterns previously unsuspected, in being handed unimagined equipment to address what arises, in the beauty and power of words.

The sheer pleasure of meeting new voices and ideas and possibilities, having the world become more coherent in some subtle or enormous way, extending or filling in your map of the universe, is not nearly celebrated enough, nor is the beauty in finding pattern and meaning. But these awakenings recur, and every time they do there's joy.

3

As a reader I roamed free. As a would-be writer, it was more complicated. In my teens and well into my twenties, I mostly encountered the literature of heterosexual men, where the muse or the beloved or the city they explored or the nature they conquered was a woman. Throughout my teens, I wrestled with Robert Graves's *The White Goddess*, which seemed to have something valuable about trees and alphabets I could never quite extract from its erudite jumble. It's a book that seemed to assume that the poet's orientation is that of a straight man to a female goddess; it might have encouraged some young women to smile enigmatically and levy tribute, but I wanted to be a writer, not a muse.

I also struggled secretly against the men around me who were convinced that they were the artists and I was the audience. Young women like me were supposed to exist as orbital figures, planets around a sun, moons around a planet. Never stars. When I was eighteen, one man was so adamant that I was his muse that he inspired in me a vivid sense that I was literally standing atop a pillar;

I can still summon up a sense of being stranded in the hazy grayish atmosphere of nowhere. On a pillar there's nothing to do but stand still or fall. I was happy to listen and read, but I was mutely against being only a listener and reader, though all I could do about that was bide my time and build my work.

I had been clear that I wanted to be a writer since the year I had learned to read, but I hardly ever spoke of this, for fear of mockery or discouragement. And until my twenties I wasn't writing much beyond what school required, though sometimes what I wrote for school worked out well. I was reading, hungrily. Classics, reassuring books, discomfiting books, contemporary novels, popular fiction, history, myth, magazines, reviews.

There were comfortable books, and another kind of comfort in recognizing my own condition or its equivalents and analogies in others, in not being alone in my loneliness and angst. Sometimes one piece would crash into me: I still have the poem "Never Before" by Philip Levine, from the *New Yorker* in the fall of 1980 (I clipped Levine's columns and taped them together into a narrow strip, now yellowed, exactly as long as my arm, with a deeper amber where the tape joins the sections together. It looks like a bandage but reads like a wound).

It is a poem of devastation:

Never before
have I heard my own voice
cry out in a language not mine
that the earth was wrong
that night came first and then nothing
that birds flew only to their deaths

that ice was the meaning of change
that I was never a child

It spoke to me when I was very nearly a child. Sometimes when you are devastated you want not a reprieve but a mirror of your condition or a reminder that you are not alone in it. Other times it is not the propaganda or the political art that helps you face a crisis but whatever gives you respite from it.

Milan Kundera's *The Book of Laughter and Forgetting* was published in the *New Yorker* in installments the same second half of 1980 and passed along to me in a stack of magazines. The chapters were, like Jorge Luis Borges's *Labyrinths* a few years earlier, revelatory. They gave me a sense of how you could mix things, how the personal and the political could spell each other, how a narrative could be oblique, how prose, like poetry, could jump from subject to subject or take flight. Of how the categories were optional, though it would take me another decade to find my way through their walls.

I wanted urgency, intensity, excess and extremes, prose and narrative bursting against the confines. Except when I wanted reassurances. I found both. I lived so deeply in books that I felt unanchored and adrift, not particularly part of my own time and place, always with one foot or more in other places, medieval or imaginary or Edwardian. I had in that floating world a sense that I might wake up or otherwise find myself in one of those other times and places.

My literary aunt who had given me *Nightwood* had given me Jerzy Kosinski's *The Painted Bird* when I was twelve or thirteen, far too young to read about the sexual brutality and genocidal violence of the Polish peasantry as seen by a dark-haired, dark-eyed Jewish child wandering through their world, barely eluding death. It took hold of me, and so did Anne Frank's diary and other Holocaust literature. One of my recurrent anxious daydreams in my childhood and adolescence was whether I with my fair hair and skin might have been able to pass as a gentile and thereby escape the extermination that had taken all the members of my father's family who had stayed behind. It was another kind of annihilation that haunted me.

But I also had a vague sense that I might find myself somehow in a less pointedly vicious time and place, where what I had learned from books would at least partially equip me to get by. That I might wander into Georgian England or medieval France or the nineteenth-century West or some of the other places in which I had immersed myself, and some sense of this, ridiculous though it sounds, made me hesitate to cut my long hair, and I found encouragement in archaic ideas of beauty to which I thought I measured up more than I did to modern ones. In those days, it didn't seem impossible that someday someone else would be in the mirror in the morning, or the world around it would be another world. "I is another" was a phrase of Arthur Rimbaud's that I also kept handy.

Of course what I had learned from books and from life had hardly equipped me well enough to fit into the time and place I actually lived in. Long after this anxious daydream had passed by, I lived a comic version of it when I read Wordsworth's book-length autobiographical poem *The Prelude* twice in order to write a chapter of my book on walking. I was so immersed in his language—unhurried graciousness, elaborate and sometimes inverted syntax, circumlocutory ways of saying things—that my casual remarks to strangers and check-out clerks were met with baffled looks.

There's a benefit to being untethered from your own time. I think I gained a sense of how differently constituted the idea of being human, the purpose of life, the expectations and desires had been even a generation or two ago, let alone half a millennium before, of how the definitions metamorphosed, and how that meant you could step outside the assumptions of your time, or at least wear them lightly, and at least in theory not let them punish you. That being human can mean many things, in other words. At thirteen, I had read C. S. Lewis's *The Allegory of Love*, which describes the social construction, in twelfth-century France, of what would become our ideas of romantic love. That these expectations were the result of a particular time and place gave me a sense of liberation, like someone opening the windows in a stuffy room.

Despite that Lewis book, I soaked up novels' impossibly dramatic notions of love and romance and their myths of completion and ending. And I got something most women got, an experience of staring at women across a distance or being in worlds in which they barely existed, from *Moby-Dick* to *Lord of the Rings*. Being so often required to be someone else can stretch thin the sense of self. You should be yourself some of the time. You should be with people who are like you, who are facing what you're facing, who dream your dreams and fight your battles, who recognize you. And then, other times, you should be like people unlike yourself. Because there is a problem as well with those who spend too little time being anyone else; it stunts the imagination in which empathy takes root, that empathy that is a capacity to shape-shift and roam out of your sole self. One of the convenient afflictions of power is a lack of this imaginative extension. For many men it begins in early childhood, with almost exclusively being given stories with male protagonists.

The term *double consciousness* is sometimes used for black experience in a white culture. W. E. B. DuBois famously wrote in the last years of the nineteenth century (and wrote, as so many men did up through at least James Baldwin, as though all people were men or even one man) "the Negro is a sort of seventh son, born with a veil, and gifted with second-sight in this American world,—a world which yields him no true self-consciousness, but only lets him see himself through the revelation of the other world. It is a peculiar sensation, this double-consciousness, this sense of always looking at one's self through the eyes of others." Perhaps there should be another term for never looking through the eyes of others, for something less conscious than even single consciousness would convey.

DuBois's framework found an echo in John Berger's 1972 *Ways of Seeing*, when Berger imagined, with generosity and brilliance, what it was to be something he had never been: "To be born a woman has been to be born, within an allotted and confined space, into the keeping of men. The social presence of women has developed as a result of their ingenuity in living under such tutelage with such a limited space. But this has been at the cost of a woman's self being split into two. A woman must continually watch herself. She is almost continuously accompanied by her own image of herself. She has to survey everything she is and everything she does because how she appears to others, and ultimately how she appears to men, is of crucial importance for what is normally thought of as the success of her life. Her own sense of being in herself is supplanted by a sense of being appreciated as herself by another."

You depend on men, and what they think of you, learn to constantly check yourself in a mirror to see how you look to men, you perform for them, and this theatrical anxiety forms or deforms or stops altogether what you do and say and sometimes think. You learn to think of what you are in terms of what they want, and addressing their want becomes so ingrained in you that you lose sight of what you want, and sometimes you vanish to yourself in the art of appearing to and for others.

You are always somewhere else. You turn into trees and lakes and birds, you turn into muses, whores, mothers, the vessel for others' desires and the screen for their projections, and in all that it can be hard to turn into yourself, for yourself. Even reading novels by men can instill this, and it did in my case. Sometimes the women devoured to the bone are praised; often those insistent on their own desires and needs are reviled or rebuked for taking up space, for making noise. You are punished unless you punish yourself into nonexistence in this system. The system is punishment. A novel like Willa Cather's *Song of the Lark* in which the ambitious, amorous, extraordinarily talented heroine is not punished comes as a shock.

Solitude was reprieve from this endless task, but when I turned to books I often turned into a man looking at women. Looking at women as problems or trophies or mildly baleful phenomena with opaque motivations and limited consciousness probably did something to me, and so did being encouraged to identify with the man over and over again, and to live in imagination in places where women were just ornaments in the margins or trophies or broodmares.

In my case, this meant identifying with male protagonists, with the Jim of the almost womanless *Lord Jim* and Jim Carroll's self-anointing stud junkie in *The Basketball Diaries* and with Pip rather than Estella in *Great Expectations*, and all the grail seekers and ring bearers and western explorers and chasers and conquerors and haters of women and inhabitants of worlds where women were absent.

And the task of finding one's own way must be immeasurably harder when all the heroes, all the protagonists, are not only another gender but another race, or another sexual orientation, and when you find that you yourself are described as the savages or the servants or the people who don't matter. There are so many forms of annihilation.

But there were some I craved. When I read, I ceased to be myself, and this nonexistence I pursued and devoured like a drug. I faded into an absent witness, someone who was in that world but not anyone in it, or who was every word and road and house and ill omen and forlorn hope. I was anyone and no one and nothing and everywhere in those hours and years lost in books. I was a fog, a miasma, a mist, someone who dissolved into the story, got lost in it, learned to lose myself this way as a reprieve from that task of being a child and then a woman and the particular child and woman I was. I hovered about in many times and places, worlds and cosmologies, dispersing and gathering and drifting. A line by T. S. Eliot, the first poet whose work I got to know, comes to mind: "prepare a face to meet the faces that you meet." Alone, immersed in a book, I was faceless, everyone, anyone, unbounded, elsewhere, free of meetings. I wanted to be someone, to make a face and a self and a voice, but I loved these moments of reprieve. If *moments* is the word: they were not intermissions in a normally sociable life; they were the life itself occasionally interrupted by social interludes.

There is something astonishing about reading, about that suspension of your own time and place to travel into others'. It's a way of disappearing from where you are—not quite entering the author's mind but engaging with it so that something arises between your mind and hers. You translate words into your own images, faces, places, light and shade and sound and emotion. A world arises in your head that you have built at the author's behest, and when you're present in that world you're absent from your own. You're a phantom in both worlds and a god of sorts in the world that is not exactly the one the author wrote but some hybrid of her imagination and yours. The words are instructions, the book a kit, the full existence of the book something immaterial, internal, an event rather than an object, and then an influence and a memory. It's the reader who brings the book to life.

I lived inside books, and though it's often assumed that we choose books to travel through them to get to the end, there were books I took up residency in, books I read again and again and then picked up and opened anywhere just to be in that world, with those people, with that author's vision and voice. Jane Austen's novels, but also Ursula K. Le Guin's Earthsea books, Frank Herbert's *Dune*, eventually E. M. Forster, Willa Cather, and Michael Ondaatje, some children's books I returned to as an adult, and early on novels that don't have much standing as literature. I roamed freely in them, knowing the territory in all directions, and familiarity was a reward as strangeness might be in a book read once just to find out what happened.

I would not call books an escape if that meant that I was only hiding out in them for fear of something else. They were glorious places to be, and they set my mind on fire and brought me in contact with the authors themselves, indirectly in their fictions, directly in the essays and journals and first-person accounts that I gravitated to as I came to understand that my own vocation was going to be essayistic nonfiction.

I swam through rivers and oceans of words and their incantatory power. In fairy tales naming something gives you power over it; a spell is some words you say that make things happen. These are just concentrated versions of how words make the world and take us into its heart, how a metaphor opens up a new possibility, a simile builds a bridge. They let me listen to conversations and thoughts that went deeper and expressed more than most people could face-to-face.

But they were not warm, they had no bodies to meet my body, and they would never know me. There was nonexistence in living through books as well as many other existences and minds and dreams to inhabit and ways of expanding one's own imaginative and imaginary existence.

4

It is as easy to decide to be a writer as to decide to have a piece of cake, but then you have to do it. I moved into that beautiful apartment as I was in my final semester of my undergraduate education at San Francisco State University. It was an intense spring: I was working to support myself and taking nineteen units of classes, helped along by a handful of prescription speed in the form of little yellow pills that had been the only gift given me by the man I'd been dating before I moved.

I graduated as I turned twenty, and then realized that the world and I were not ready for each other. I got a desk-clerk job a pleasant walk from home in a small hotel, out there on the edge of the Castro District in those last years before AIDS would change everything for the gay men who thronged the streets of the neighborhood. I stayed there for a restorative year of catching my breath and looking around and not being desperate for time or money. The job left a lot of time to read behind a rolltop desk, in between checking guests in and out and taking reservations by phone and mailing confirmations and sometimes making up beds or breakfast trays. There were troubles—a lecherous elderly boss, the sorrows of a refugee housekeeper whose husband beat her, a few crises with customers—but mostly it was peaceful.

After graduation, I had realized that though I had learned to read, I had not learned to write, or to do anything better than sales and service work for a living. In those days before nonfiction was considered creative and taught in writing programs, I applied to the only place that I could afford and that made sense to me, the Graduate School of Journalism at UC Berkeley, and was admitted. The writing sample I submitted was a blithely amusing (but laboriously typed) account of an encounter with a group of women at a punk club when I was eighteen or nineteen.

The women had invited me to audition for a movie that turned out to be an attempt to repeat the process whereby they and the quadriplegic man who'd be the film's director had groomed a teenage girl via sex work to obey him. They wanted to repeat the process only with a movie camera and with me; sex with him, the women explained, was part of the deal, and he chimed in by spelling out "show me your tits" on his communication board with his pointer. Servitude and obedience were described, of course, as liberation.

The Pygmalion myth, whereby a woman is turned from insensate sculpture into a living being, happens much more frequently in reverse, as a story of women who don't need help being fully alive and aware confronted with the people who want to reduce them to something less. Perhaps in turning the encounter into an essay, I had affirmed my capacity to think, judge, speak, decide, and maybe thereby to make myself. I was going to graduate school to get better at those things.

I didn't fit into the school well when I started it a few months after

I turned twenty-one, because most of the other students seemed to want to be what the school wanted us to be: investigative journalists whose holy grail was the front page of the *New York Times*. They were more sophisticated about politics, older than me, consciously low key in their appearance while I was still flamboyantly punk rock in thrift-store black and crayoned-on eyeliner. I wanted to be a cultural writer, an essayist, though what exactly I wanted was not nearly as clear as what I did not want. I wanted to be pretty much what I eventually became, but there were not a lot of models and examples that I knew then, just inclinations and excitement from the work of writers like Pauline Kael, George Orwell, Susan Sontag, Jorge Luis Borges.

What I learned there was immeasurably valuable. I was trained in resourcefulness in how to find out things, in ruggedness about meeting deadlines, in how to organize a story and verify facts. I was instilled with a commitment to precision with language and accuracy with data and a sense of responsibility toward readers, subjects, and the historical record that still matters to me.

Just before my first year began, the hotel in the Castro was sold, and the new owners laid me off after promising not to. Desperate, I talked my way into a waitress job at an Italian restaurant just opening, but my inability to remove corks without a graceless struggle was one of the reasons that didn't work out. Had I been better at sales and service my fate would probably have been worse. I trudged over to UC Berkeley's work-study office, disclosed my plight, and got my chance to apply for one of the jobs they orchestrated and partially financed. I pursued one at the Sierra Club and one at the San Francisco Museum of Modern Art, both of which were offered to me. I went with the museum, for reasons I no longer remember; I still work with both institutions from time to time.

That the gracious women in pearls and pumps who made up the research/collections department hired me still surprises me. I had gone for my interview wearing a baggy men's suit from a thrift store, pants held up with a cowboy belt, and my new rockabilly haircut, short on the sides and frothing into a pompadour on top. (I had thought I'd look tough and androgynous when I chopped off my long hair, but instead it curled when it was relieved of its own weight; toughness was an ideal I aspired to without success, at least as an aesthetic.)

Those women must have seen something in me, because they soon promoted me from rote filing work and set me to do serious research. I was there every Tuesday and Thursday for the next two years, and full time in the summer between my first and second years of graduate school. It was the best job I ever had. The museum, which had been the second modern art museum in the country, was preparing for its fiftieth anniversary in 1985, and I was helping with the catalogue of the permanent collection's highlights that would be published on the occasion, the first time I produced content for a book. I was researching major works of art, and it was the beginning of an education in modern and contemporary art.

I was handling Matisses, Duchamps, Miros, Derains, and Tamayos (I don't think I worked on anything by a non-male artist, though I was excited by San Francisco art historian Whitney Chadwick's recuperation of the reputations of the women surrealists and the emergence of Frida Kahlo as a cultural icon in those years). I was putting together a dossier on each piece—sales and ownership history, exhibition history, a bit of information on the life and work of the artist at the time of its creation, contextual material on related works, and more. For two years I wandered in and out of storage spaces, file rooms, library stacks, typing up data on a big electric typewriter, corresponding by letter with scholars, solidifying the biographies of a few dozen works of art and broadening and deepening my own sense of art history.

I worked directly with paintings in the course of documenting the labels and inscriptions on their back sides. I went into the basement to catalogue Marcel Duchamp's *Boite-en-Valise*, a little suitcase with miniatures of his major works of art, and the brief covetous moment I had—my boyfriend at the time loved his work—faded when I realized that every work of art lives in its context, and a stolen work of art has to exist outside of it, silenced, unable to circulate in the conversation from which it emerged. That storage basement had other lessons to impart: it contained some art that would probably never be shown again—paintings and other items that had seemed significant in their time but been written out of history or never written into it, odd trends and faded heroes, movements that had lost their sheen, detours from the official road of art history, a windowless room of orphans and exiles.

I also spent hours in the hushed back room full of files from the era of Grace McCann Morley, the museum's inspired, forgotten founding director, and it was then I fell in love with archives and the task of assembling a history out of fragments. I noticed a drawing by Matisse in a letter to her and had it moved from correspondence files to the art collection. I wandered through the history of many artworks like a traveler, learning about the world around them, coming to recognize landmarks I could return to. I worked on a painting by the German expressionist Franz Marc—a mountainscape he had repainted after he'd been to Paris and seen the brand-new thing that was cubism: I had it X-rayed to show the old painting underneath, and I found the data to change the title. To play a role in the writing of art history, even with this one tiny act, was electrifying.

Since Morley, all the directors of that museum have been men, but a few ranks below, women seemed to run everything. I worked under a kind patrician woman out of a tiny office in the library who taught me my job, and I often wandered over to consult the dashing, graying, gravel-voiced longtime librarian Eugenie Candau in her own office, and sometimes I scrounged from her wastebasket the exhibition postcards she discarded. I was ravenous for images. It was a second education as valuable and formative as the one I was getting across the bay at the university.

One day I saw a work of art by Los Angeles artist Wallace Berman that captivated me. It was a grid repeating an image of a hand holding a transistor radio with images bursting out of the radio's speaker, a piece about pop culture and mysticism with a few Hebrew letters scattered on it. In my naïveté, I went to find the book that I assumed existed on this extraordinary creator. There wasn't one then, though there was a slender exhibition catalogue surveying his work. I didn't yet know that I would write that book, or a version of it, some years later. I picked Berman as the subject for my thesis, though it was unconventional for a journalism student to focus on something so far from the news and the realms of news. Berman had died in 1976, having destroyed the recording of the only interview known to have been conducted with him, so there was a lot to reconstruct from archives and interviews with members of his circle. The coincidences that led me to the museum that led me to the image that led me to the project make me grateful for my failure at opening wine bottles.

5

Though I was browsing at City Lights bookstore and researching the Beat poets for that thesis, and interviewing some of them, I encountered my fellow San Franciscan Diane di Prima's work only later, including her declaration "You cannot write a single line w/out a cosmology." Writing is often treated as a project of making things, one piece at a time, but you write from who you are and what you care about and what true voice is yours and from leaving all the false voices and wrong notes behind, and so underneath the task of writing a particular piece is the general one of making a self who can make the work you are meant to make.

It formalizes the process everyone goes through, of making the self who will speak, of settling on what values and interests and priorities will shape your path and your persona. You have to find out what kind of tone you are going to take, how you pitch your words, whether you're going to be funny or grim or both. Often what emerges is not what you intended; it turns out you're someone else who has other things to say and other ways to say them (what gets called "a voice" is at the outset like some person you don't know very well arriving at the front door with a different focus and tone than you expected). You discover what ethics are implicit or explicit in how you describe the world, what ideas of beauty you are going to pursue, what your subjects are, which means what you care about, all those things labeled style and voice and tone behind which lies a question of self.

I went back to di Prima's declaration in her famous "Rant." Further down, the poem continues:

> There is no way out of the spiritual battle
> There is no way you can avoid taking sides
> There is no way you can not have a poetics
> no matter what you do: plumber, baker, teacher
> you do it in the consciousness of making
> or not making yr world

The voice that came out of me when I spoke in social settings and often even to a single friend wore a thousand pounds of armor and was incapable of saying anything direct about emotions, which I was barely feeling or feeling through so many filters I hardly knew what was spinning me around. But the voice: it was the voice I'd grown up around and learned to emulate and then to promulgate, a voice that strove to be clever, cool, sharp, and amused, to shoot arrows with precision and duck the arrows that came back or pretend they hadn't stung. It relied on jokes and quips that were often cruel in a game where anyone who was hurt or offended by those jabs was supposed to be lacking in humor or strength or other admirable qualities. I didn't understand what I was doing, because I didn't understand that there were other ways to do it, but that didn't mean it wasn't mean-spirited at times. (Later, I discovered that scathing and mocking reviews were the easiest and most fun kind to write, but I tried to write them only about much-lauded successes.)

There was another kind of humor, or rather a ponderous wit, that was convoluted, full of citations and puns and plays on existing phrases, of circling around, far around, what was happening and what you were feeling. It was as though the more indirect and referential your statement, the further away from your immediate and authentic reaction, the better. It would take me a long time to understand what a limitation cleverness can be, and to understand how much unkindness damaged not just the other person but the possibilities for you yourself, the speaker, and what courage it took to speak from the heart. What I had then was a voice that leaned hard on irony, on saying the opposite of what I meant, a voice in which I often said things to one person to impress other people, a voice in which I didn't really know much about what I thought and felt because the logic of the game determined the moves. It was a hard voice on a short leash.

That voice isn't just in your conversations, it's inside your head: you don't say that hurt, or I feel sad; you run angry tirades about why the other party is a terrible person over and over, and you layer on anger to avoid whatever's hurt or frightened underneath, until it's certain that you don't know yourself or your weather, or that it's you who's telling the story that's feeding the fire. You generally don't know other people either, except as they impinge on you; it's a failure of imagination going in and reaching out.

But that was just the stories within. The stories I wanted to write and the person who would write them were not yet born. I knew who I admired, but not who I was. You cannot write a single line without a cosmology. I had so much work ahead of me, and I did it slowly, in stages. I was many different writers along a road on which my various books and essays are milestones or shed snakeskins. In journalism school I learned to write straightforward reports, though my first teacher there resented my inability to write the flat prose that was often taken for journalistic objectivity, which even then I saw as a masculine voice. I could keep opinions at bay if I tried hard, but not adjectives.

The television show *Dragnet*, which was old even then, opened every episode with a hard-boiled man's voice flatly declaiming, "The story you are about to see is true. The names have been changed to protect the innocent." It was like the prose of Ernest Hemingway, which my first college English professor had insisted was the pinnacle of good writing, that stripped-back, clipped, terse language that was also about masculinity and its parsimonious words packed in silences. It was a voice policing many things, and leaving a lot unsaid in the same way that the ironic poses favored by my family did. The tone that we were supposed to deploy as journalists sounded to me like that tone, though at least we were allowed to quote people who might be more expressive and emotional.

I wanted language that could be simple and clear when the subject required it, but sometimes clarity requires complexity. I believe in the irreducible and in invocation and evocation, and I am fond of sentences less like superhighways than winding paths, with the occasional scenic detour or pause to take in the view, since a footpath can traverse steep and twisting terrain that a paved road cannot. I know that sometimes what gets called digression is pulling in a passenger who fell off the boat. I wanted English to be an instrument on which many kinds of music could be played. I wanted writing that could be lavish, subtle, evocative, that could describe mists and moods and hopes and not just facts and solid objects. I wanted to map how the world is connected by patterns and intuitions and resemblances. I wanted to trace the lost patterns that came before the world was broken and find the new ones we could make out of the shards.

Some Uses of Edges

—·····◆◆◆◆◆◆◆◆·····—

I

t's written in pencil on a large sheet of now-yellowed news-
print whose bottom half has the wide-ruled lines for beginning writers, and I'm pretty sure it's my first essay, from first
grade. In its entirety, it reads, "When I grow up I will never get
married." The illustration on the top half shows a man in a red shirt
whose black hair wraps like a nimbus around his circular head and
a yellow-haired woman in a flounced purple skirt. "Get married
with me," he says in a cartoon balloon, and she says, "No, no."

It's comic and horrible, a sign that I was looking at my mother's
life and thinking that whatever I did, I would try to not do what she
did, because she so clearly felt trapped and powerless in a violently
miserable marriage. I am the offspring of a victim and her victim-
izer, of a story that couldn't be told at the time. Most conventional
stories for girls and young women ended in marriage. Women vanished into it. The end. And then what happened and who were
they? The fairy tale "Bluebeard" is about a woman who finds out, by
disobeying his orders and using the forbidden key to unlock the

torture chamber full of her predecessors' corpses, that she's married a serial killer, whose intent to kill her is whetted by her knowledge. It's an unusual fairy tale in that she survives and he does not.

I'd just rejected the principal story for women, and I'd soon elect to try to put myself in charge of stories. That is, the same first year of literacy, after a brief period when I wanted to be a librarian because they spent their days with books, I realized someone actually wrote each book, and decided that that's what I wanted to do. Such an unwavering goal from early on simplified my path, though the task of writing is never simple. Becoming a writer formalizes the task that faces us all in making a life: to become conscious of what the overarching stories are and whether or not they serve you, and how to compose versions with room for who you are and what you value.

But when it comes to writing, every chapter you write is surrounded by those you don't, every confession by what remains secret or indescribable or unremembered, and only so much of the chaos and fluidity of experience can be sifted and herded onto pages, whatever your intentions and even your themes. You're not carving marble; you're grabbing handfuls of flotsam from a turbulent river; you can arrange the detritus but you can't write the whole river. Though so much of the stories of those who came before is missing, I understand now how the deep damage passed down from my grandparents formed my parents, and how public histories shaped our private lives in various ways. I've lived long enough to know five generations of my family and to see how the weight of history that happened two generations before me—hunger, genocide, poverty, the brutalities of emigration, discrimination, and misogyny—still has consequences two generations after me. I've written my parents' obituaries on that little desk from the woman who didn't die and lived in the peace that came after they were gone. I'm uninterested in the brutalities of childhood in part because that species has been so dwelt upon while some of the brutalities that come after have not.

Threads are usually the wrong metaphor for things that branch and fork and lead in many directions, but maybe the way many fibers are twisted into a thread means that following a thread should mean unraveling it or recognizing the individual strands. For example, after graduate school, I got hired by a little art magazine as an editorial assistant and I quickly became the assistant editor, by title, and more or less the managing editor in terms of what I actually did. I learned a lot of things there, from the rules of copyediting to how to direct a staff older than me to how to put together a publication to quite a lot about contemporary art, particularly California art. I wrote obituaries, reviews, some features, and a few investigative reports, and endless bits of filler, and with the magazine's owner coedited the dozen or so often abysmally written pieces we received each Monday until they were ready to send to the printer on Thursday afternoons. It was an all-woman office in downtown Oakland I worked at for three and a half years after I graduated from Berkeley, and it was a haven of calm and routine, and a place where even though the magazine was not a great magazine I learned great things.

I am endlessly thankful that my path to writing detoured through visual art. It was an arena in which artists were asking questions that went down to the very foundations and reached in all directions. Art could be almost anything, which meant that every premise was open to question, every problem to exploration, every situation to intervention, and I came to understand visual art as a kind of philosophical inquiry by other means. I learned from paying attention to the work of some artists, from conversations with others, and from collaborations with yet others, and from wandering through the texts often then referenced in the art world, the French philosophers and feminists, the postmodernists, and other dense things from which useful ideas could be gathered.

When I was a couple of years out of graduate school, still working at the magazine, I went to a slide talk by the photographer Linda Connor about landscape and gender. She had collected a lot of amusing images of men pissing and teeing off golf balls from high places, and she postulated, with this evidence and a lot of more serious contemporary photography, that men photographed space, but women photographed place. It was a funny, tough, insightful talk about how we represent place and what our place is supposed to be. I'm not sure either of us would now agree with the neatness of categories she sorted the world into then, but she stood there as someone with a key to a door I wanted to unlock and pass through.

I cooked up a couple of assignments to write about her so I could learn more. She was sixteen years older than me, in her prime, with a great halo of curly hair and a big circle of friends, a house full of curios and objects she'd picked up around the world, and nonchalance about cooking dinner for forty at a time or carrying through deserts and mountains her enormous view camera that made eight-by-ten-inch negatives. Her black-and-white prints were made on printing-out paper, an archaic light-sensitive—but not too sensitive—paper she could just lay under the negatives and leave out for hours to develop in the sun of her back garden, in what felt as domestic an act as hanging out the laundry.

SOME USES OF EDGES

She was traveling while I was on deadline to write about her,
so I asked if I could talk to her while coming along on her drive
to New Mexico. It was a tutorial in how to go on a road trip, and
she was a brilliant guide to diners, campsites, motels, to when to
detour and when to cover distance. We pulled into the grand old
pile that is the La Fonda Hotel in downtown Santa Fe one afternoon in early August, where she'd arranged for the artists Meridel
Rubenstein—another landscape photographer I knew slightly—
and her husband, the painter Jerry West, to meet us. We had come
all this way like an arrow flying through the air past many other
things to hit exactly this target that was the table in a shadowy al-
cove in the honeycombed hotel, where Meridel's assistant, Catherine Harris, was also seated. We ordered margaritas, and Meridel
and Jerry invited me to come stay at the house Jerry had built on
the prairie outside town on land his parents had homesteaded
during the Great Depression.

And Catherine—a darkly beautiful young artist with tawny
shoulders in a sleeveless white jumpsuit—and I began talking. We
became close friends, perhaps best friends, for years after, had a falling out that kept us apart for years, then I dreamed of her one night
and ran into her on the street in the morning—she had moved to
San Francisco at that point—and we exchanged phone numbers
and picked up where we left off. I am not a proper memoir writer in
that I cannot reconstruct a convincing version of any of our conversations, even the long one last summer in the house where she lives
in Albuquerque with her husband and two kids and some dogs.

Those conversations were analytical, confessional, usually punctuated with gales of laughter, taking up the pieces of our education,
the ideas and templates and pigeonholes, and trying them on to see

how they fit our urgent personal needs. I do remember how amused we were one time as we rejected the earth-mother ecofeminism of the moment by noting that our mothers—squeamish, anxious, repulsed by human bodies and their smells and secretions—were not in the least like nature. And of course in those early years we talked about the boys we were pursuing or entangled with or disentangling from, but that was mixed in with books, politics, ideas, projects, and plans.

When we were eating breakfast in the yard of Meridel and Jerry's house a day or two after I first met her, Catherine told me, as she watched me untangling my damp hair, about going to the pueblo corn dances two days before and seeing women with hair down to the hems of their long dresses, and then about the job she'd had photographing the students at a Native American school and how one of the girls told her about cutting off her own long braids. The story found its way into an essay of mine, because Catherine was told the child "was ashamed to go home afterward, and when she did, her grandfather chided her gently, telling her that her hair contained all her thoughts and memories."

I had published journalism and reviews, but I was exploring a more intimate, lyrical kind of writing, one where the spirit guiding the connections and trajectory was intuitive and associative rather than linear or logical. The results were short and dense, though this essay was a thicket of stories about hair and its power. Catherine's anecdote gave me its conclusion. Then she made a photograph of me sitting and looking back at her with my own hair hanging to my waist, against one of Jerry's unfinished adobe walls, the concrete scraped into rough ridges so the mud would adhere.

We began a correspondence by mail and then email and launched a series of adventures, driving back and forth together between

Santa Fe and San Francisco, doing projects together and encouraging each other as she came into her own as an artist and then a landscape architect and I kept writing. And so out of the lecture of Linda's that I wandered into so casually came some ideas about place and landscape, friendships, eventual collaborations with all four of these artists, a cherished friendship with Catherine in particular, and an anecdote about hair as a repository of memory. And a return to the region in which I spent the first two years of my life, a place I fell in love with as an adult for its sense of deep time on the ground and constant change in the sky.

Your life should be mapped not in lines but branches, forking and forking again. Meridel introduced me to people who became significant friends in New Mexico, and I've returned there nearly every summer since, and that summer landscape became one of my great joys. Jerry deepened my understanding of the place he's now spent more than eighty years in and paints with such love. Catherine moved to New York for a few years, and I first visited the city as an adult to stay with her (as a young art critic, I'd thought that I was probably supposed to move there to plunge more deeply into the art world or climb its career ladders, and when my writing began to be about western places, I was hugely relieved that I'd written my way out of that fate).

Perhaps you could tell a story the way children play hopscotch, returning to the beginning and going a little further each time, tossing your token into another square, covering the same ground in a slightly different pursuit each time. You can't tell it all at once, but you can cover the same ground a few different ways, or trace one route through it. In 1988 I went to the Nevada Test Site for the first time, to join the immense antinuclear activist gatherings there that my younger brother was already helping to orchestrate. That was a path I would travel far on, meeting extraordinary people, and finding another route into the landscapes I craved, into a world far beyond San Francisco. A path, or a gate.

Out there in the Nevada desert one day the photographer Richard Misrach met me, walking up with his huge view camera slung casually over his shoulder. His big color photographs of places of violence and destruction in the American West had a major impact then and were the subject of some controversy, from people who thought he was glorifying the wrong things, perhaps because they believed that only the good should be beautiful, while he was interested in the tensions of a hideous beauty and the demands it made on us when the ethical and the sublime or beautiful are at odds. He became another artist whose work quite literally made me think—about that conflict between beauty and morality, the invisibility and pervasiveness of certain kinds of violence, the legacies of the conquest of the West, and what he often called "not the representation of politics but the politics of representation." Later in the 1990s, I wrote the text for a couple of his books.

The support of these artists who were so much further along in their work and their sense of purpose and self gave me the confidence to move on from regarding myself as a critic and a journalist to trying on being a writer. Or rather they told me that's what I was when they told me they wanted to work with me, and reminded me that that had been my original goal I had somehow backed down from. Criticism and journalism had felt like subordinate forms of writing in which you were always serving a subject and operating by constraining rules. To be regarded as a writer freed me to feel that anything was possible and everything was available.

One day an artist I knew told me that Ann Hamilton was making an installation in an industrial space in the city, and she was looking for volunteers to help, so I wandered down to Capp Street Project, a former auto-detailing garage in the Mission District. Ann had become recently and suddenly famous for her immense, ambitious installations, often involving vast accretions of small objects and materials, enlivened by performers present throughout the duration of the exhibition. She was only five years older than me, full of midwestern steadiness and modesty, but also an extraordinary confidence manifested in the sheer scale and effort of her works, at a time when many young women were making what felt like miniatures.

Ann had converted much of the budget for her show into pennies, because she was ambivalent about the lavish budgets for such projects. The 750,000 pennies that $7,500 dollars translated into would be put on display, then scraped up and taken to the bank to be washed, counted, and converted to currency that could be donated to an education project. In the meantime, she was filling much of the floor of the space with a vast rectangle—forty-five feet by thirty-two feet—of pennies laid down, one by one, on the cement floor "on a skin of honey." Honey was the adhesive, but also a way of referencing another system of circulation than money, of putting together how bees store their labor and how we do. Ann had been much impressed by a bricklayer in her childhood, and then gone into fine art through textiles. She was interested in how a small gesture repeated enough made something large, and so three quarters of a million gestures laid down that many bits of currency in a shining skin of money.

Somewhere during that process, I got down on my knees and started laying out pennies, and a while later Ann ended up doing the same next to me and we began to talk. We laid the coins out without an attempt to make a pattern, but the natural variation in the long lines made them take on a texture like waves or snakeskin scales, and they shimmered in the light, and the smell of honey rose up from the floor. I don't know what had changed, but at the beginning of the 1980s I had hardly been able to connect to anyone, and I hadn't found my people or the conversations I dreamed of. At the end of the decade, I could and I did.

The piece Ann made with many hands' help was called *privation and excesses*, and at the far corner of the great carpet of cash was a performer, a person in a white shirt sitting with a wide-brimmed felt hat full of honey in her lap. The performance consisted of wringing one's hands in the honey and staring off into the distance—of maintaining a calm disengagement from the viewers. To include a performer meant that the grammatical tense of the piece was in the present of making and doing, rather than the past tense of made and done. Later on in other pieces of hers, the performers would be undoing something, unraveling, or erasing, so that the work was being unmade as well as made for the duration of the exhibition.

Later on, Ann took some of the pennies converted back into practical currency and gave it to me to write an essay about the piece. But before that she asked me to be one of the performers. Thinking back it seems enchanted that she invited me into both an ongoing conversation and into silence. To do the latter job, you sat in a straight chair for three hours, looking ahead, blessedly instructed to ignore all the visitors' questions about what the art meant. There was a pen with three sheep in it behind the sitter, and the sounds and smell of the sheep, as well as the smell of the honey and the pennies, were part of what you absorbed when you took on the task.

As a child you're told not to get sticky, not to play with your food, not to make a mess, and sinking your hands up to your wrists in honey was a wonderful transgression against all that, as well as a sensual pleasure. If you were the first sitter of the day, the honey was cold and a little stiff at the outset, but it warmed up from the heat of your hands and began to flow. You can hold a double handful of honey, though it will drip, but your job in that artwork was not to hang on to it but to let it move, to lift it out of the hat and let it trickle back, to keep it moving while the rest of you stayed still and silent and looked ahead with a thousand-mile stare.

Restless, nervous, impatient by nature, I had thought I would have a hard time sitting still for three hours, but I found that the instructions protected me from my own sense that I should be available to supply information (and people did come up and demand explanations of the show) and that I should at every waking moment be busy and productive. I found instead that I resented the person who replaced me when I was the first performer of the day or the gallery staff person who told me to wrap it up when I was the last.

One day many years later those hours sitting still with my hands in warm honey came back to me as a recollection of the calmest moment of my youth, a few hours of pure existence as sweet as the honey stuck under my nails, a moment of being rare among all the busyness of doing and becoming.

2

Hopscotch: back up a little, cover the same ground again. My father had died while traveling on the other side of the world in the first days of 1987, and with his death it became safe enough to thaw out a little and to open up what had been closed. I was finally having emotions in response to events from long before, as if they had been something frozen into the ice in that bleak earlier era, and because I could finally classify the events on my own terms as cruel and wrong. Later that year, my longtime boyfriend moved to Los Angeles, the rest of my family was particularly difficult for me, and I was living off unemployment insurance from the job I'd been laid off from after I left the art magazine, some savings, small sums dribbling in from reviews and essays in local magazines, and some work as an office temp in businesses around the city.

I decided that when you had nothing left to lose you were free, and that what I wanted to be free to do was write a book about the community I had discovered—and many of whose members I had met—when writing that graduate-school thesis about Wallace Berman four years earlier. I sent a book proposal to City Lights Books and it was accepted in early 1988, and I got my first book advance, for $1,500. I had wanted to write books since shortly after that first-grade anti-marriage essay, because I loved books more than almost anything, because I regarded them as a kind of practical enchantment, and the only way to be closer to that enchantment than reading them was writing them. I wanted to work with words and see what they could do. I wanted to gather up fragments and put them in new patterns. I wanted to be a full citizen of that ethereal otherworld. I wanted to live by books and in books and for books.

It was a lovely goal or rather orientation when it was far away throughout my childhood and teens and college years, but when it came time to do it—well, the mountain is beautiful in the distance and steep when you're on it. Becoming a writer formalizes something essential about becoming a human: the task of figuring out what stories to tell and how to tell them and who you are in relation to them, which you choose or which choose you, and what the people around you desire and how much to listen to them and how much to listen to other things, deeper in and farther away. But also, you have to write. I had published a lot of essays and reviews by that time, but a book—it was like going from building toolsheds to a palace.

That first book began with that work of art I had seen one day in 1982 on a wall by the staff offices of the San Francisco Museum of Modern Art. It was a square black-and-white collage by Wallace Berman, a grid of sixteen images of a hand holding a transistor radio, four across, four down, the same hand and radio each time with a different image where the speaker should be on the radio.

Among the images were human figures, including a nude, a football player, a frail figure that might be Gandhi, a human ear, a bat hanging upside down, a hypodermic, a gun, and the same sinuous snake twice on the bottom row. They were negative images, so that everything seemed a little dreamily unnatural. It was as though each image was a sound translated into sight, as though each was a message, a warning, a proclamation, or a revelation. Or a song. A few Hebrew letters written in white on the black background insisted that the mystical and esoteric could coexist with pop culture, that some of the old divides were unnecessary or illusionary. It had been made with an early version of a photocopy machine called a Verifax. It was titled *Silence Series #10*.

Berman was, like my father, the child of immigrant Jews, raised in Los Angeles. Unlike my father, he was slight, subtle, choosing to live a life on the margins of society and the economy, first in the swing and jazz scene in L.A., then among mystics, dropouts, artists, and rebels. He had, as he'd predicted, died on his fiftieth birthday—been hit by a drunk driver in a truck as he drove in his sports car on the winding, narrow road to his birthday party in one of the canyons on the edge of Los Angeles that evening in 1976. After being prosecuted for obscenity for his first art exhibition in 1957, he'd chosen to keep a low profile. My original title for the book was *Swinging in the Shadows*, taken from a postcard he wrote to the painter Jay DeFeo, in which he told her that he was going to go earn some money and swing back into the shadows again, but my publisher overruled me on that.

For the thesis I had pieced together Berman's life from what people around him had to say, what the art itself told me, from archives and oral histories, exhibition catalogues and old postcards and letters that people still had on hand. In so doing I realized a number of things, including that there had been a California avant-garde in the 1950s that had been overlooked in official histories, a series of coteries and communities involved in film, poetry, visual art, esoteric and non-Western spiritual traditions and practices, and mind-altering drugs. An avant-garde that helped give rise to the counterculture of the sixties, a realm of experimentation and rebellion and reinvention. This was what I wanted to write a book about, not one artist, but a community of artists.

Back then, cultural history was supposed to be a linear business that had unspooled in Europe and then in New York, and California was a despised hinterland, a place in which nothing much was supposed to have happened. Someone once sneered at a friend of mine doing a thesis on western history at Yale that *People in California don't read books*, as though all the poets in the mountains and the scholars in the cities and the indigenous storytellers in the ninety-nine native California languages from the desert southeast to the rain forests of the northwest boiled down to one empty-headed sunbather on a hot beach. In 1941, Edmund Wilson wrote, "All visitors from the East know the strange spell of unreality which seems to make human experience on the Coast as hollow as a troll nest where everything is out in the open instead of being underground." In 1971, Hilton Kramer wrote in the *New York Times* that the San Francisco Bay Area was characterized by "the absence of a certain energy and curiosity, a certain indispensable complexity and élan" and dubbed the style of one of the artists "Dude Ranch Dada," though dude ranches were mostly a phenomenon of the intermountain West, many hundreds of miles away. Things seen small at a distance lack detail, and growing up when I did you saw

California through eastern telescopes when you saw it at all. That era of disdain and dismissal had not yet ended when I was a young writer.

In the course of writing that book I worked out for myself why I was grateful that we shared a border with Mexico and faced Asia and were farther from the influence of Europe that was supposed to convey legitimacy, and that I suspected imparted conventional-izing impulses, and I came to understand how many writers, from Mark Twain to Seamus Heaney to Alexander Chee, had come here to get free of something and gone back changed. Many years later a student who'd just moved to the Bay Area from New York (and had before come from Mumbai) relayed her distress to me at no longer being in the center of things, with the implication that centers are what matters. I went home and thought about the value of margins.

I'd written about them in my work on hope and social change, because I'd been following how ideas move from the shadows and the fringes into the center and how much the center likes to forget or ignore those origins—or just how those in the floodlights can't see what's in the shadows. The margins are also where authority wanes and orthodoxies weaken. My first education in how all this worked came from Wallace Berman, who had consciously chosen to live on various edges—economically precarious, subcultural, often literally on the edge—homes perched on stilts in the canyons of Los Angeles and the salt marshes of the Bay Area. From those locales he had been influential for people who plunged into the limelight—poets, artists, actors such as Dennis Hopper, Russ Tamb-lyn, and Dean Stockwell. One sign of Berman's influence is his in-clusion in the collage that is the album cover for the Beatles' 1967

Sgt. Pepper's Lonely Hearts Club Band; another is his small role as a sower in another iconic artwork of the era, Dennis Hopper's 1969 film *Easy Rider*. (The name of Berman's hand-printed magazine was *Semina*, from the Latin for seeds and semen, and he was a sower of seeds—that's literally what he does in his cameo in *Easy Rider*—but also a cultivator of the seeds others had sown.)

To delve into his life and milieu meant interviewing, first for the thesis, then for the book, people who I still thought of as grown-ups—adults intimidatingly older than me. They were my parents' generation but they were people who had lived their lives as great adventurers, taking risks, not chasing stability, and not regretting it. My parents were, even after decades in the middle class, so governed by old Depression-era fear of poverty that their lives were cramped and cautious. These extravagant peers of theirs provided a fine alternative model of how to live your life. When I began that book four years after I graduated, I didn't know that I myself would never really get around to getting a job again. I would have endless work, and write a lot of books, and a lot more essays and articles, and I'd do some activist work and some teaching, but I'd never really go back to being an employee with a salary and a boss.

The North Star is so far away from earth that it takes its light more than three hundred years to reach us, and even the light from the closest star takes four years. A book is a little like a star, in that what you read is what the author was passionately immersed in long before, sometimes only because of the time it takes a book to be written, edited, printed, and distributed. And because often the time it takes to make a book means that it represents the residue of interests that preceded the writing. By the late 1980s new interests were eclipsing the ones that came before; I was engaged in a new way with ideas about nature and landscape and gender and the American West.

This first book was about revisiting and completing something significant that I had found years before. I focused on six artists—three from Southern California and three from the Bay Area—whose lives and work and ideas had overlapped as they became friends and sometimes collaborators in the 1950s: Jess (who'd abandoned his surname when he left science for art and a life as an openly gay man when that was a superhumanly bold thing to do), Jay DeFeo, Bruce Conner, George Herms, Wally Hedrick, and Berman. Each of them had chosen in various ways to lead a low-profile life, to find out what making art could mean and what a life full of it could be and then making it and living it. Conner, Hedrick, and DeFeo had opportunities to go to New York and become stars, but they declined the opportunity.

Their idealism was underwritten by the affluence of the era and their own frugality, by white flight that left cities full of cheap housing, and wages high enough that couples and families often lived tolerably off the income from one part-time job. Even in the 1980s, the kind of freedom to come and go, to stop paying the landlord for months and then find another pleasant place to live, to drop in and out of the economy seemed like the strange customs of an ancient free people. The artists I wrote about had moved on the edge of Beat circles or passed through them, and the story often told about the Beats as a group of male writers from the East morphed into something larger and more interesting that included these visual artists and experimental filmmakers and the poets who were part of other movements, notably what got called the San Francisco Renaissance, including Jess's life partner, Robert Duncan, Jack Spicer, and Michael McClure, who moved through many worlds.

I learned from these characters that before you can make art you have to have a culture in which to make it, a context that gives it meaning, and people from whom to learn and to whom to show your work. Through short-lived galleries, tiny magazines, screenings, poetry readings, friendships, they made culture happen among themselves—among themselves not because they were exclusionary, but because they were excluded. I came to understand some general principles about how cultures evolve and shift and how ideas migrate from the margins to the center. They overlapped with jazz musicians, rock bands, drug dealers, biker gangs, gay subcultures, social experiments, countercultural heroes. They had that camaraderie I still sometimes recognize in small towns and conservative communities, where the outsiders stick together because their differences from each other are insignificant in the face of their differences from a hostile mainstream.

Research is often portrayed as dreary and diligent, but for those with a taste for this detective work there's the thrill of the chase—of hunting data, flushing obscure things out of hiding, of finding the fragments that assemble into a picture. Your shards are stories, facts, manuscripts and letters, photographs, old newspaper clippings, the bound volumes of magazines no one has opened in years, something someone says to you in an interview they have not said to anyone else quite that way. For my early books, I was amazed to have neglected topics to write about that seemed significant to me, and it came to feel like an advantage that I was in a place that had been so overlooked and dismissed.

Some of my early research adventures were comic. When I was working on my thesis, I kept calling up the actor-director Dennis Hopper in New Mexico, hoping to talk to him about Berman, and he kept answering cordially, saying he'd be happy to talk, but could I call back later, until, dozens of calls later, the phone bills grew alarming and I gave up. I didn't try again when I turned the project into a book, though he was living in Los Angeles, because I had been so terrified by his performance in the film *Blue Velvet*, but his assistant was helpful to me and got me six prints from his original negatives—Hopper had been a talented photographer in his youth—to use in the book.

I even got, from a bohemian with his dentures out in whose little room I spent a pleasant hour, a mumbled account and an unpublished photocopy of a letter a friend sent him about the October 1955 Six Gallery reading that became famous because there Allen Ginsberg read "Howl" aloud for the first time. The drama of that breakthrough for one poet overshadowed the proto-environmental poetry that Michael McClure and Gary Snyder read that night. The accounts generally said little about the location as well, an artist's co-op gallery where Hedrick was a principal, as well as the instigator of the reading. It was a delightful document that let me see how the event had felt to a participant before it and the official Beats at it got mythologized.

Nonfiction is at its best an act of putting the world back together—or tearing some piece of it apart to find what's hidden beneath the assumptions or conventions—and in this sense creation and destruction can be akin. The process can be incandescent with excitement, whether from finding some unexpected scrap of information or from recognizing the patterns that begin to arise as the fragments begin to assemble. Something you didn't know well comes into focus, and the world makes sense in a new way, or an old assumption is gutted, and then you try to write it down.

In a way, this has been my life's work, the pursuit of patterns and the work of reconnecting what has been fractured, often fractured by categories that break a subject, a history, a meaning into subcompartments from which the whole cannot be seen. While there's a kind of expertise that comes from microscopic focus, I would often pursue the patterns that reveal themselves across broad areas of space or time or culture or categories. The art of picking out constellations in the night sky has cropped up again and again as a metaphor for this work.

This was true to a degree of the subject of this first book, whose story had been largely missed by the linear narratives of art history, film history, and literary history. The relationship between film, poetry, and visual art, between drugs, esoteric and non-Western philosophies, political dissent, and queer culture, between members of a funky coterie that could be described as avant-garde were it not also catalytic in a counterculture, was what mattered. My artists weren't very well documented beyond those oral history interviews, and they weren't very visible, though most of them—particularly DeFeo and Conner—got a lot more attention afterward.

The artists' own works were often a kind of collage, literally: of the six artists central to the book, Jess, Berman, George Herms, and Bruce Conner were known primarily for their collages and three-dimensional assemblages. Jay DeFeo was, like Wally Hedrick, primarily a painter, and one whose work often featured a powerful solitary form, but she too ventured into collage on many occasions, mixing painting and photography and found material. Collage makes something new without hiding the traces of the old, makes a new whole out of scraps without erasing the scrappiness, emerges from an idea of creation not as making something out of nothing, like God on the first day or painters and novelists, but as making something else out of a world already exploding with images, ideas, wreckage and ruin, artifacts, shards, and remnants.

Collage is literally a border art, an art of what happens when two things confront each other or spill onto each other, what conversations arise from the conjunction of difference, and how differences can feed a new whole. For these artists it was also a poverty art, one of scrounged materials from the Victorian houses being knocked down in the black neighborhood around them, the detritus of thrift stores, scraps from magazines. Conner even made his first films out of found footage because he couldn't afford a camera, and then settled into this recontextualizing as his chosen genre, or mixed found and new footage to make films influential for their inventive editing and pacing.

Putting together this picture of my part of the world as it existed not long before I arrived in it was a paradise of ideas and pattern recognition, perhaps more so because it was the first time I had done so on such a scale. That I was getting to know the past of my own city and region meant that places I had passed through were acquiring new layers of meaning. I was writing about the world up to the point when I had been born into it, and it was foundational work for moving forward in that world. I was writing a cultural history that gave my own part of the world significance and possibility I had not seen before. I was becoming an expert on a subject, and that too had its rewards.

Diving Into the Wreck

1

When I wrote that book, I conducted a number of interviews with straight male subjects who thought I might be a groupie of sorts, and demonstrating a deep knowledge of their milieu was one way to dispel some of that: I'm not excited to meet you, I'm excited to reconstruct how it all came together in 1957, and I have most of the pieces but would like to ask you a few things. I remember one of them inviting me to sit on the sofa with him, and putting my tape recorder between us as a tiny barrier; another who seemed frisky with anticipation of some sort of frolic we might engage in; and years of sexual harassment from Bruce Conner, who I tried to keep at bay in part by addressing him as Uncle Bruce and his wife as Aunt Jean, a reminder of, among other things, our age gap. The conduct of the frisky artist seemed to come from something very familiar to me, a sense that since young women are nobody, nothing you do with them is on the record, which was disconcerting to run into while I was making the record of his life and achievements.

As part of my research, I paid to have several short films screened for me at the Pacific Film Archive and Canyon Cinema, but there was one I didn't see at the time but had read about often in the literature. Works of art you have only read or heard about take on their own dimensions, and often such a work takes on a life in your imagination before you see the real thing. My imaginary film of joyous liberation withered when I finally saw *Pull My Daisy*. Codirected by the painter Alfred Leslie and the photographer Robert Frank, it had a voice-over by Jack Kerouac.

The film begins with a woman opening the drapes and picking up after her husband: "Early morning in the universe. The wife is getting up, opening up the windows. She's a painter and her husband's a railroad brakeman. . . ." She never acquires a name, never paints, but is only the wife, the one who gets the kid breakfast and dispatches him to school, tends the house, and represents all the things the men are escaping or avoiding and definitely disdaining. She doesn't seem to be there when the overcoat-clad Allen Ginsberg, Gregory Corso, and Ginsberg's lover Peter Orlovsky burst into the flat and begin drinking and partying. The men come and go with booze and cigarettes, smitten with themselves and their notion of themselves as winsome. Ginsberg rolls on the floor like a puppy at one point, another of them cuddles a jug of wine like a teddy bear, Kerouac's voice-over says, "Let's play cowboys," and they riff on what kinds of cowboys they are.

The central drama unfolds in the evening, when a bishop invited by the wife arrives with his mother and his sister. He's a young man in a flashy white suit, and we never find out what he's the bishop of, though clearly he's supposed to represent all things orthodox. The gang of poets are rude to him, confident that their rudeness is another mark of their liberation. But the bishop's stodgy mother is played by Alice Neel, the painter whose work—mostly portraits and nudes—even in the 1930s was fearlessly original and transgressive. The brakeman/husband's diligent, shrewish wife is played by the starkly gorgeous Delphine Seyrig, who went on to become a major film star and then a major voice for feminism in France.

So two great women artists, one in her prime, one at her start, play dreary, nameless nobodies and appendages: literally a wife, a mother. (The railroad brakeman, whose name—Milo—is often invoked, is played by the painter Larry Rivers.) When the Beat poets, who are referred to by their real names, interrupt Neel's organ playing with jazz we're meant to understand that she too represents convention and they improvisation and the cool stuff. And then all the men, except the bishop who had departed earlier with his family, go out into the night to play, and the wife stays home with the dishes and the kid. I'd always heard of it as a celebration of liberation, but you could only read it that way if you imagine that you're one of the poets, not one of the women. If you're one of the women, you've just been told you're no one, except a mantrap and a bitch and a baggage.

How do you make art when the art that's all around you keeps telling you to shut up and do the dishes? What do you do with culture heroes who have had beneficial effects but not for you or people like you, whether it's personal malice or categorical scorn? The Beats loomed over my generation, or codified versions of them did. My formative years had been peppered with men who wanted to be Kerouac, and who saw that job as the pursuit of freedom, and saw freedom as freedom from obligation and commitment, and, when it came to art, stream-of-consciousness spontaneity, art freed up from composition and plan. There were so many of them, including the handsome, sweet one I went to my first Nevada Test Site antinuclear action with in 1988 and the arrogant indigent college acquaintance who several years earlier had crashed with me and my gay roommate, devouring the contents of the refrigerator and scribbling condemnations of us in the journal he left lying open.

I did like some things about Kerouac's prose style, just not the gender politics of the three men who were most often meant when people talked about the Beats. Those politics had contaminated Kerouac's *On the Road* for me when I was a teenager. I got as far as the protagonist's encounter with Terry—"the cutest little Mexican girl" who he later calls "a dumb little Mexican wench" with "a simple and funny little mind." And then the protagonist—a lightly fictionalized Kerouac—takes off and leaves her. As in the film, a woman is a stationary object, a man is a pilgrim and a heroic wanderer. He's Odysseus; she's Penelope, but Homer took an interest in the gallant struggle of the woman who stayed home. It seemed to me that I would never be the footloose protagonist, that I was closer to the young Latina on the California farm who gets left behind, and halfway through I put the novel down. The book was going to go on without people like me, and I was going to go on without it.

Years before I took on the Beats as a subject, I'd had an even more intense sense of erasure at the opening for an exhibition of Ginsberg's photographs. The walls were hung with dozens of inscribed black-and-white prints of his male friends in various places, having adventures, having each other, having the world as their oyster, and then a print or two of Peter Orlovsky's mentally ill mother and sister sitting on the edge of a bed, sad, stranded, hopeless. They were, as I remember it, the only women in the show. As in *On the Road* and *Pull My Daisy*, they were immobilized objects in a context where freedom and mobility were equated.

I became silently furious, back in the day when I had no clear feminist ideas, just swirling inchoate feelings of indignation and insubordination. A great urge to disrupt the event overtook me; I wanted to shout and to shout that I was not disrupting it because a woman is no one, to shout that since I did not exist my shouting did not exist either and could not be objectionable. I was, in that room, that time, clear and angry about my nonexistence that was otherwise mostly just a brooding anxiety somewhere below the surface. But I remained silent; contributing to the sense of women as burdensome, crazy, angry, intrusive, unfit was not going to help.

Often a phenomenon that appears revolutionary because of some new feature can be seen as drearily conventional because of others that stood out less at the time. The men considered the principal Beats were opening up space to be queer or bisexual, to experiment with drugs and consciousness and non-Western spiritual practices and philosophies, to try to find white literary equivalents to the great experiments of black jazz musicians then, to make of improvisation and the American vernacular and pop culture something truly of this time and place, not a dressed-up deference to Europe.

Also, most of them despised women, and in this respect they were entirely of their time and place, the woman-hating American 1950s, whose mainstream literary lions were dubbed a few years back the Midcentury Misogynists. Watching *Pull My Daisy* one more time made me go back to Leslie Fiedler's 1960 book *Love and Death in the American Novel*. The American canon was, in his reading, men's literature, and though he disparaged most of the men he considered, he disparaged women by not considering them. He noted that the overarching theme of *Huckleberry Finn* and *Moby-Dick* and some of James Fenimore Cooper's frontier novels was the love between a white and a nonwhite man and that this literature took place in the wide-open American spaces where men were free to roam and women were absent. "As boys' books we should expect them shyly, guiltlessly as it were, to proffer a chaste male love as the ultimate emotional experience—and this is spectacularly the case." A little less chaste in the Beats, but no less boyish.

And later on he notes of the women in these books, "Only in death can they be joined in an embrace as pure as that of males. The only good woman is a dead woman!" I didn't shout that day, but I did have my revenge on another one of the holy trinity of the Beats one February evening in my early twenties. I had just begun to publish, so it must have been early 1984, and the woman who was my editor at a little music and culture magazine told me that Survival Research Labs, a punk performance trio of men who made menacing dystopian machines that moved and spun and lurched at the audience and self-destructed with flames and explosions, was hosting a birthday party for William Burroughs. Then she told me (though I don't know if it's true) that a noted woman artist had cut her hair off and made herself androgynous so that she could work with him and that everyone at the party would—as at pretty much all punk parties in that era—don the tough-guy drag of dark jeans and leather jackets and women would play down their gender and everyone would stand around looking angsty and rugged.

That spring Luc Sante's scathing essay on Burroughs in the *New*

York Review of Books made a deep impression on me. He quoted Burroughs as saying to an interviewer, "In the words of one of a great misogynist's plain Mr. Jones, in Conrad's *Victory*: 'Women are a perfect curse.' I think they were a basic mistake, and the whole dualistic universe evolved from this error." Sante wrote, "He associates women with the most repressive aspects of Western culture, and he has no sexual need for them; q.e.d., they are superfluous and impedimental. When the tricky problem of reproduction is eventually solved, women will simply be wished away." Burroughs had also shot dead Joan Vollmer, his wife, on September 6, 1951, and though there are conflicting versions of how and why he asked her to put a glass on her head for him so he could "play William Tell," what's clear is that he pointed a gun at her and shot her through the forehead and she died.

A young man I spent time with in my twenties, my boyfriend's younger brother's best friend, was more enamored of Burroughs than anyone else I knew, though a lot of people I knew revered the old writer back in the day when he was seen as one of the godfathers of punk culture. The young man was gay, cut off from his Texas family, trying to find his way, a talented musician, but a devotee of the idea of the derangement of the senses through drugs as the royal road to artistic genius. That derangement came up from Arthur Rimbaud a century before and evolved into another fixture of counterculture, the idea that you got to your creative self by getting fucked up, that some genius is lurking behind the inhibitions and you just have to let the genius out to do its thing without plan or discipline or structure.

Burroughs was seen by some of the young people around me as exemplary of all this, and he had spent a lot of time taking a lot of drugs, buffered by a family allowance and an apparently iron constitution. The young man I knew had neither. I remember with affection one evening with him when he was hallucinating and wielding colored markers, trying to draw on paper (and album covers) and scrawling directly on the floor of my apartment. Then it's with sadness that I remember him becoming more and more of a meth addict, and then a homeless person walking barefoot in dirty jeans on Market Street unable to recognize me. He was cared for by a kind older man for a while, and then I heard he jumped off the Golden Gate Bridge, a sweet and talented young soul, dead of many things, including the prevailing mythology.

My editor and I went to the party at the Survival Research Labs industrial space under a freeway overpass in chiffon dresses. She was full figured, with long blond hair, and wore something beautiful and flowing with lots of cleavage; I wore what I thought of as my dead ballerina outfit. It had probably been a child's dress and then moldered for years in some basement before I found it in a thrift store. It had a tiny bodice with rows of yellowed lace, strapless, though I'd improvised a strap out of one of the half-torn-off rows of lace, and a full, calf-length skirt made of shredding petals of gauzy fabric that hung down in points.

I've often found that I want to live up to my outfit, and a festive outfit produces a festive spirit, and so she and I went shouting with laughter, flirting and weaving and waving our arms and wafting perfume and smiling lipstick smiles and looking around freely with our painted eyes among the people who were standing about being so deadpan they seemed to have turned to stone. The man accompanying Burroughs was taking photographs and he wanted to photograph us with the guest of honor and there was a moment when at his urging she and I came at Burroughs from either side and he shrank into his already withered self in what appeared to be horror. I've always described him as looking like a slug between two saltshakers in that moment. It was very satisfying, and then we moved on.

2

Writing is an art; publishing is a business, and in starting my first book I was launching myself on a series of adventures with small and large publishers. The writing was me alone in a room with ideas, sources, and the English language, which went well, overall. The publishing was me negotiating with organizations that always had more people and more power and sometimes acted as my advocate and collaborator and sometimes as my adversary.

One winter evening not long ago, my friend Tina and I went to see *The Post* at a little movie theater out in the west of San Francisco, where the sky is darker and the wind is stronger and everything seems a little dreamier. The movie told two intertwined stories, about the *Washington Post*'s decision to report on the Pentagon Papers, the material leaked by Daniel Ellsberg to make it clear that the Vietnam War was based on a lie, and the way that Katharine Graham, who had recently taken over as publisher when her husband died, simultaneously seized hold of her business and herself, sweeping aside the men who condescended to her as she swept aside her own self-doubt about her qualifications to take power and make decisions with world-changing consequences.

We enjoyed the drive, and the crisp night air, and before that the popcorn and the vintage Republican decor and wardrobe of the cinematic Ms. Graham and the scenes of printing presses running. When we exited into a very black night, I somehow found myself talking about my own early struggles with publishing. It had been a long time since I'd recalled how bitter my early endeavors to put out books were, in their own small way, or rather how fervently men had sought to prevent me from publishing. I was lucky in that I overcame the obstacles they erected, but I presume others did not. And now I can see how white the world of publishing was and is, and that though some doors slammed because of my gender, others remained open because of my race.

Some of the damage was funny in its own way. There was an editor who one day changed things at random in the manuscript of my first book, so the French artist Niki de Saint Phalle became Niki de Saint Paul, iconic to ironic, 1957 to 1967. The reason for this desultory sabotage I do not know, but when I fought it I was treated as though I should take random errors inserted into my manuscript more in stride. Another editor, I recall, wrote me a scathing note about that book's inconclusive ending; he'd lost the last chapter of the manuscript, but did not imagine the error was his. The process of producing the book dragged out an extra year because of my inexperience and inability to advocate effectively for myself against odd interventions like that.

And then there was Lawrence Ferlinghetti, the figurehead of that publishing house and enterprise. It is now more than thirty years since I signed a book contract with City Lights Booksellers & Publishers, and during those first few years I was very often in the editorial offices in the back of the top floor of the bookstore, which I've returned to often as a browser, a friend of some of the staff, and occasionally a reader at events. In these decades Lawrence Ferlinghetti, who floated around there regularly, has never spoken a word to me, including under circumstances where speaking to me would be the normal thing to do. I was never sure whether it was that he wouldn't or he couldn't. Sometimes I thought that he might possess a sort of Venn diagram in which City Lights authors or historians were not a group that intersected with young blondes, so that I was categorically nonexistent.

Once, when I had been working with City Lights for more than two years, Ferlinghetti came with City Lights' editor in chief to a book party I'd helped organize for my friend Brad Erickson's activist handbook. A week later Brad and I met at City Lights and Ferlinghetti came down the little staircase next to the famous bookstore's front door and looked at the two of us, one he had met once briefly, one he was publishing and had crossed paths with dozens of times over the past few years, and said to us, "Hi, Brad." I didn't particularly want to be pals with him, but it is normal for your publisher to say hi to you. Thinking back, that peculiar business makes me believe that my urge, years earlier, at the Allen Ginsberg photography show, to shout about my nonexistence had a basis.

Some of it was less funny. Talking to Tina in the winter air, I remembered for the first time in years how another powerful old man attempted to destroy that first book altogether. John Coplans had been a cofounder of *Artforum*, the most daring of the major American art magazines, when it began life in San Francisco in

1962, and he had written about Bay Area artists for the magazine. In the 1980s, he had some success as a photographer. His subject was his own sagging, hairy, aging, nude body depicted up close in black and white as a sort of monolith that took up all the room in the picture.

When my book appeared in 1991, Coplans had a lawyer write a letter to City Lights accusing me of libel. Wally Hedrick, one of the six central subjects of that first book, had painted American flags starting in 1953, and one way or another he'd lost or destroyed all the paintings that might've had some minor status as landmarks of American art, since New York painter Jasper Johns was famous for having begun painting American flags slightly later. (He painted a lot of them black to protest the Vietnam War.) One of Hedrick's paintings, I wrote in my book, "survived until 1963, when (according to Hedrick) the art critic John Coplans borrowed it from a ten-year survey of Hedricks's work and never returned it. He had asked to bring it to a woman interested in buying it, and the work has never been seen since."

Coplans claimed that not only did this make him out to be a thief, but that he'd never met Hedrick. As I recall it, the lawyer's letter suggested that if we destroyed all copies of the book, no further action would be taken. The desire to casually annihilate the years of work and the moment of arrival that a first book represented was stunning. It didn't help that, so far as I could tell, the editor who received the letter seemed to think it quite plausible that I had gotten my facts gravely wrong. I rarely seemed to be regarded as in possession of much competence and credibility in those days, whether it was about a personal interaction or about history.

I'm still in the habit of amassing evidence to back me up, and that's what I did then: I went to the SFMOMA museum library and photocopied a pile of material about the two men's published conversations and collaborations back in the day. My editor, I believe, forwarded the material to the lawyer. All the copies of my book were not destroyed, though it had a very quiet life and is now out of print. One of the two write-ups attributed authorship of the book to poet and critic Bill Berkson, who'd written a very gracious foreword, opening with a quote by Mina Loy: "The common tragedy is to suffer without having appeared."

In 2008 I wrote an essay called "Men Explain Things to Me" that contains the sentence "Credibility is a basic survival tool." In a way, credibility is also my profession or at least part of the necessary equipment of any writer of nonfiction. I had to fight for it in the beginning. That is, I had to fight to convince others, in both personal and professional life, to grant me the capacity to perceive events with a reasonable degree of accuracy, and the frequency of this experience sowed self-doubt in me, so the struggle was not only with others.

It is not always possible to say that a given weather event is due to climate change, but that climate change shapes the trends is clear, and the same can be said of discrimination—that this particular event may or may not be due to someone's attitudes about people in your category, but the cumulative effect suggests a pattern. Looking back now, it seems that had I not lived in a culture where the threats against me and the violence against women around me were real and pressing and the disdain of those writers who were so lionized in my youth wasn't so scorching, then these actions against me might have seemed a series of unfortunate, unrelated incidents.

My second book was a very different book, and it had an auspicious beginning: I sent a proposal on a Monday in 1991 to Sierra

Club Books, was called by an editor on Tuesday, and met with him on Wednesday. The book contract came soon afterward. I sold my battered Datsun B210 and spent part of the $12,000 advance on a used white Chevy S10 pickup truck with a camper shell to better pursue my research across the West. My life had changed while I was writing *Secret Exhibition*, and if that first book laid the foundation for me to understand recent and local history just before my era, this second book would be a broader and deeper inquiry into the American West and its myths, wars, blind spots, wonders, criminals, and heroines.

This book, *Savage Dreams: A Journey into the Hidden Wars of the American West*, was about how invisibility permits atrocity. The war at the center of the book's first half was at the Nevada Test Site, where the nuclear wars generally regarded as a terrible thing that might happen someday were in fact happening at the rate of about one nuclear bomb detonation a month from 1951 to 1991, more than a thousand in all, with dire impact on the local environment and the human beings downwind. The second half of the book was about Yosemite National Park, where the Indian wars widely regarded as something bad that happened long ago were going on in the present by other means against Native people who had not, contrary to what was then conventional belief, disappeared, vanished, reached the end of the trail, set off into the sunset, or been the last of their kind. Native people had been rendered invisible by representations or rather nonrepresentations—in signage, in the more visible of its two museums, in land management practices, and in the depiction of Yosemite by environmental organizations and artists as an uninhabited wilderness recently discovered by white people and a place people only belonged as visitors.

That is, I was arguing that the wars of the future and the past were overlapping in the present, and that they were largely unrecognized because of how we thought about things like war, and the West, and nature, and culture, and Native people. I was the beneficiary of a revolution of ideas under way about all those things. Native people were asserting that they had never gone away, never given up on their rights, never forgotten their history, and that the land had a history, a history of cultures that were not separate from or destructive of nature. It was a revolutionary realization for non-Native people like me, a recuperation after what has sometimes been called symbolic annihilation, a term for the nonrepresentation of a group—a gender, an ethnicity, an orientation—in the popular culture or the arts and official versions of their society or region. Among other things, it undid the tidy nature/culture binary that was so widely used to organize ideas back then.

My editor was encouraging. But when the manuscript was finished, in 1993, he sent it out for peer review to two men who'd written Western histories. One was Evan S. Connell, whose own history of Custer and the Battle of Little Bighorn was experimental enough that I thought he'd have a positive reaction, but he seemed to regard my book as incoherent and objectionable, which was disappointing, but fine as an opinion. The other guy, who'd written a book about a national park, was upset about my ideas on Yosemite, insisting on reading what I described as cultural blind spots as intentional conspiracies whose existence he denied. The book's epigraph was James Baldwin's spectacular sentence "It is the innocence which constitutes the crime," meaning that it's not cunning but obliviousness, willful or otherwise, behind so much brutality. In a long, indignant letter, he accused me of, among other things, "intellectual dishonesty" and a "hidden agenda," and he wrote, "I have taken the liberty of copying my remarks to a few respected colleagues, among them park officials in Yosemite."

I wrote him back that my agenda was not hidden and that "I spoke with my former professor Ben Bagdikian about the matter today, and he condemned the action as wrong. Bagdikian, former ombudsman for the *Washington Post*, currently a professor of journalism at UC Berkeley, and a national authority on journalistic ethics, said that although it is customary to circulate unpublished academic writing within academic circles for review, the circumstances here are different: your attack on my book was sent not to impartial authorities but to concerned parties who also happen to be governmental officials, an unheard-of compromise of journalistic independence for writing dealing with social and political issues. A likely effect of such an act is to create pressure on the publishers to withhold publication." Recruiting a powerful man was, like throwing published data into a conflict, another chess move to compensate for my own lack or sense of lack of credibility in the conflict. And I pointed out to my editor that in raging about my sins of interpretation—and only those sins—this reader had apparently found no factual errors worth mentioning.

Credibility is a basic survival tool. The book went through the usual editorial processes, and then in the fall of 1994 it was in print. Because it was in part about nuclear weapons and the campaigns against them, and because my younger brother was an antinuclear activist and a kind and supportive person, he helped organize a speaking tour across the American West, using his networks to set me up at colleges and radio stations and activist groups, and joined me on the 7,000-mile journey in my Chevrolet truck. We stayed with friends and acquaintances, mostly his, all the way; in Dallas, our host politely asked us what route we took there from San Francisco, and I was pleased to be able to reply to him, "Via Seattle."

Sierra Club Books assigned an in-house publicist, a tall blond man who became more and more peculiar as I tried to work with him. It became impossible to reach him by phone or to get him to return calls, but he emailed me that he had booked me in bookstores across the West as part of that grand tour and gave me dates that fit the schedule. I'd been ignored when I'd complained to other people at the publishing house about him, and I'd gotten the impression, again, that they considered me overwrought and my concerns baseless. When we were already out on the road, I got suspicious and found a pay phone from which I called the first bookstore he was supposed to have booked me into. I found out he'd never contacted it. I made more calls.

He was a liar. None of the events he'd claimed to have scheduled me into existed. When I did radio interviews it turned out that the interviewers hadn't received the copies I'd asked him to send, so they had no clue what we should talk about. He had, one way or another, decided to bury my book. The book remained far more invisible than it might have been otherwise, and our tour was full of gaps and dead spaces we could have filled ourselves if we'd known what he was doing. I thought *Savage Dreams* was an important book, or at least a book trying to look at important, urgent things in new ways. (Its title, which I regret, was after a charismatic monster named James Savage, who initiated genocidal wars in the Yosemite region in pursuit of gold-rush profit.)

If someone had listened to me when I began to distrust him out loud, his malice or incompetence might not have had such an impact. During those first few years in publishing I was writing history and being regarded, as young women often are, as not particularly capable of bearing witness even to everyday interactions. I was reading in public and being unable to make myself heard by my publishers. That evening with Tina after the movie, when I told her about Coplans and the rest, I realized for the first time how much it all felt like a genteel, disembodied version of the annihilatory rage I'd met on the streets a few years earlier. These incidents seemed intended to tell me that this was not my place and in it my voice would not be heard.

Now, I feel lucky to have gone through all that before even the internet, let alone social media, had come along. We know the malice there is distributed by gender and race, and that a lot of collective online labor is put into making people who aren't white or male or straight or cisgender shut up and go away. If they aren't silenced altogether, they pay this tax on having a voice, they do the extra work to overcome the obstacles that keep things unequal. On a few occasions, as I've watched people try to whip up hate campaigns against me on social media, I've thought that had they tried to do so at the outset rather than decades into my life in print, their efforts might have had an impact that would be harder to ignore or override (though maybe I would've also been posting publicly about my peculiar encounters with men in publishing and finding solidarity there).

Mostly we hear from people who survive difficulties or break through barriers and the fact that they did so is often used to suggest the difficulties or barriers were not so very serious or that what doesn't kill you makes you stronger. Not everyone makes it through, and what tries to kill you takes a lot of your energy that might be better used elsewhere and makes you tired and anxious. The process of writing and publishing nonfiction convinced me of my own credibility and capacity to determine what was true and just more than anything else did, and that made me able to stand up, sometimes, for myself, or for others.

O ften, when a woman says that bad things have happened
to her or to women and the perpetrators were men, she's
accused of hating men, as though the reality of those
events is not relevant, only her obligation to be sunny no matter
what is, or as though the fact that not all men are awful outweighs
the reality that some are in ways that impact her. Often what a
woman says is weighed for what kind of woman that makes her and
whether she's still pleasing to others rather than its factual content.
My twenties included a wonderful boyfriend who was with me
from my twenty-first birthday until my late twenties, and my
younger brother who drew me into his activism and supported my
work that became increasingly intertwined with this activism. And
gay men, as friends and as a huge cultural force in the city I lived in
and models of what else being male could mean. And what being
human could mean.

Every day, when Jay DeFeo was suffering from the lung cancer that would kill her in late 1989, she would call up Ed Gilbert, he told me years later.

"Ed, what are you wearing?" she would ask him. I remember his performance of her voice as soft and ethereal, floating on the air like the smoke from one of her cigarettes or the plumes of one of the objects she drew with whirling charcoal lines. Ed, the director of one of San Francisco's leading art galleries, Gallery Paule Anglim, now Gallery Anglim Gilbert, would describe that particular day's sartorial splendor and then she would say, "Thank you. I feel so much better," and hang up. They had that conversation over and over, almost daily, as she declined, and each time she seemed to find pleasure in it.

He was golden-skinned, with close-cropped hair, and his magnificent form always reminded me of the sleekly powerful Oscar statues. His wardrobe was vast, full of elegant outfits by small and local and sometimes major designers and vintage picks, statements that had wit and wryness and sometimes glamour in many colors, with the shoes to go with it. Contemplating the wonder that was Ed, dressed, I came to recognize that though looking amazing is usually thought of as either a mildly despicable self-glorification or a straightforward strategy to access sex, it can be a gift to the people around you, a sort of public art and a celebration, and, with wardrobes like Ed's, even a kind of wit and commentary.

People watching is one of life's great pleasures, and I felt fortunate to live among drag queens and the Sisters of Perpetual Indulgence, the AIDS activist group and parodic sororital/fraternal organization launched at the end of the 1970s, among people who took any excuse to costume—in a city of parades and street parties and festivals for Dia de los Muertos and Halloween and Gay Pride and Chinese New Year, among subcultures with their particular styles from punk to lowrider to hip-hop to the many people remaking gender to suit themselves and signifying it by personal style and body language. And the eccentrics who belonged to no clan or were a tribe of one, back when people lived in public more. The city back then felt like an unending carnival of self-invention, of every walk down the street as potentially a parade, and some people worked harder at performing for it than others, but there was always plenty to see, from rainbow-colored Mohawks to tattered ball gowns, and sometimes both together.

Perhaps the reprieve Ed's wardrobe provided a dying woman was one of the ways I was learning that who you are and what you do and make and wear and say can be a contribution to people around you, that many of the most valuable gifts are not direct or material or measurable. That even how you live your life can be a gift to others. Being around gay men liberated me, because liberation is contagious. I learned so much from them, benefited in so many ways, enjoyed myself so immensely. Of course the things I'm saying are not about all gay men, only about my encounters with the ones who delighted me and the ones who became my friends.

For thirty years, I lived a short walk from the Castro District, and even before I'd been a San Franciscan, I'd gone to see movies at the Castro Theater, one of the few grand movie palaces that hasn't been demolished or converted to a multiscreen cinema. I've seen hundreds of films in its dim, majestic cavern. Sitting there for film festivals, for classic Westerns and musicals, for the annual film noir festival, for the AIDS documentary *We Were Here*, for scads of Tarkovsky and Antonioni and the feature film about Harvey Milk that let us see the theater we were sitting in on the screen, I learned from the murmurs and sighs, the cheers and groans and snickers, to read the homoerotic subtexts, to note the camp, to call out the hate in the old films and the botched ideas in the new ones. Gay men taught me to read closely, to celebrate and critique, and to share in the jokes, even when we were (mostly) quiet in the dark.

The way you might be proud of your city's civic architecture or teams, some of those of us who were straight were, I think, proud of our gay population back then, pleased to feel worldly about the antipuritanical realms of the bathhouses and the queer leather scene such as they were before the AIDS epidemic; sophisticated enough to banter with a drag queen or join the glorious variety of Halloween in the Castro when that impromptu street carnival was in full flower, before the college kids and other onlookers diluted it and the violence came; pleased to be in a place where events and characters flourished that might not happen anywhere else, cherishing the way the city was a magnet for people desperate to get away from the wholesome America that wanted to kill them; awestruck by the vision and heroism of some of the political leadership in the streets and eventually in office.

My first gay male friend came along when I was about thirteen, and he took me to my first drag-queen bar on Polk Street not long after, of which I remember little but the festive flutter of the queens wearing pancake makeup who sat at a little café table with us and kindly admired my childish complexion. There was a sexual geography in San Francisco, with the leather scene on Folsom Street, trans women and drag queens in the Tenderloin, gay men on Polk

Street before the vitality of that scene faded as the Castro became the new capital, and lesbian bars and clubs in North Beach before my time and then in various places around the city before they too faded away. For a while, in my late teens and early twenties, I went dancing at the Stud, a leather bar that was one of the rare places where a punk crowd and a gay crowd overlapped (and were sometimes the same people).

The gay men and lesbians around me encouraged me to imagine that gender is whatever you want it to be, and that the rules were breakable, and that the price to pay for breaking them was generally worth it and then some. The men made it clear that what troubled and frustrated me in straight men was not innate to the gender but built into the role. Or as the direct-action group Queer Nation put it in the stickers they scattered around town in the early 1990s, "What causes heterosexuality?" They modeled for me the radical beauty of refusing your assignment, and if they did not have to be what they were supposed to be, then neither did I.

Across the United States and elsewhere are people who imagine and desire and sometimes demand homogeneity as a right, who claim coexistence compromises or menaces them. I wonder about them, about what it must be like to be the kind of person who expected to dominate a country and culture forever and to find safety in homogeneity and danger—mostly imagined, or of a metaphysical variety—in heterogeneous society. I was white, but I grew up the daughter of a liberal Irish Catholic and a Russian Jew in a conservative and sometimes anti-Semitic neighborhood, a book-besotted kid in an anti-intellectual town, a girl in a family of boys. I didn't think there were a lot of people exactly like me or that they would ever amount to a majority population anywhere. In a homogeneous

RECOLLECTIONS OF MY NONEXISTENCE

environment, I always felt I stuck out in ways that might be punished; to be in a mixed crowd was safer as well as more rewarding. And living in a white-minority city, I came to think "like me" meant people who loved the same things or held the same ideals.

There are so many ways to disappear. And some were never allowed to appear in the first place. San Francisco supervisor Harvey Milk's aide and close friend Cleve Jones, who's had a major political career of his own since, wrote in his memoir *When We Rise,* "I was born into the last generation of homosexual people who grew up not knowing if there was anyone else on the entire planet who felt the way that we felt. It was simply never spoken of. . . . Being queer was sick, illegal and disgusting and getting caught meant going to prison or a mental institution. Those who were arrested lost everything— careers, families and often their lives. Special police units hunted us relentlessly in every city and state. . . . By twelve years old I knew that I needed a plan. The only plan I could imagine was to hide, never reveal my secret, and if discovered, commit suicide."

Those formative years of mine were transformative years for queer culture, and most of the men I knew had some version of Cleve's journey through secrecy and shame to find friends, lovers, and a place in the world, or at least in the city, or at least a few neighborhoods there. From the 1970s protests against antigay legislation through the White Night riots after Milk was assassinated by a conservative ex-cop to the ferocious activism of ACT UP and Queer Nation into the 1990s, it was a politically charged place. It was both a center of the AIDS crisis and of organizing to respond to it, from the work of the Sisters of Perpetual Indulgence to educate about safe sex to ACT UP and Queer Nation to Cleve's AIDS memorial quilt project, a project so massive that the last time it was displayed in its entirety, in 1996, it covered the entire Mall in the nation's capital.

I watched the AIDS crisis as a bystander passing through a Castro that suddenly had bulletin-board notices and gay newspaper articles about a strange new disease, then skeletal men teetering along the sidewalks, memorial displays, protests and marches. I was close to one man, the artist David Cannon Dashiell, from the time his longtime partner Barry died of an experimental AIDS drug to his own death almost four years later. David gave me Barry's black leather motorcycle jacket after my own was stolen, and I wore it for years, back when leather jackets were a kind of uniform for people like us.

David was devastated by Barry's death, but his partner's life insurance policy let him have things he'd always wanted, starting with more time to make art. He went on a shopping spree, buying and remodeling and furnishing an apartment and buying a lot of art by gay artists he admired—Jerome, Nayland Blake, Lari Pittman—knowing what I didn't, that his remaining time was brief. Even the furnishings had mordant wit; at his dining table were six steel wheelchairs upholstered with dark watered satin and fringe dripping from the arms, a wink at how the disease might disable him. We used to speed around the flat in those chairs, laughing.

His art was erudite, a project of queering existing representational systems—I still have one panel from the Tarot deck he redrew in chalk on big rounds of black paper; mine shows a man from above, his muscular form drawn in a few swift lines, his nipples tiny spikes on his strong chest. David was tall, willowy, with pallid skin, an archly aristocratic manner, and much delight in decadence and transgression. I was who he called the night his HIV turned into

AIDS. I rushed over to the glamorous flat he'd put together, bringing fruit juice, soup, and the fluffiest films I could find. Reclining in his bed in the bay window of his Victorian apartment, we watched *Picnic* with Kim Novak and William Holden, one of those movies whose over-the-top heterosexual rites were a perfect occasion for snarky remarks. We stayed up late over soup and movies, and in the morning he went to the doctor. Neither of us was equipped to talk directly about what was happening, but it happened anyway.

David fell in love again, and they toured Europe with a suitcase of clothes and a suitcase of pills. He completed his masterpiece just before he died. It was a reenvisioning of the Villa of the Mysteries murals in Pompeii, a huge installation, with life-size figures painted on eight-foot-high sheets of plexiglass: white- and lavender-complected Edwardian gay men, kissing, cannibalizing, exchanging bodily fluids; green-skinned science-fiction lesbians also engaged in transgressive erotic rites. I was witnessing his simultaneous appearance and disappearance, the former as an artist rising in ambition and visibility, the latter from the disease that killed him at forty in the summer of 1993.

San Francisco was a refuge, but far from a perfect one, and homophobic violence was a presence even here. A man named James Finn, in the course of writing about being assaulted elsewhere for being gay (and, with his powerful husband, winning the battle), noted, "When a homophobic man taunts a gay man, he almost invariably does so by comparing him in unfavorable terms to a woman." Gay men were despised for being men who had, in the imaginings of homophobes, chosen to be like women. Like women in being penetrated, when being penetrated was seen as being conquered, invaded, humiliated. Like straight women in being subject to men (though nonstraight women who were not subject to men upset them too; they upset easily).

Which means that some heterosexual men and for that matter whole societies, notably ours, imagine sex with women is punitive, damaging, adversarial, an act that enhances his status and demolishes hers. In some cultures the man who penetrates anyone or anything, including another man, retains his stature; it's the man who allows himself to be penetrated who has fallen from the status of a man (which has made it doubly hard for boys and men who are rape victims). An acquaintance told me about going home, long ago, with a college friend whose father was a Wall Street broker. The rest of the family was enjoying dinner in their lavish Upper East Side apartment when the broker arrived. Everyone fell silent, and he sat down and roared, apropos of his day in the stock market, "I fucked him up the ass." Winning over his competitor was like having sex with him, and sex is hostile and punitive at one end and humiliating at the other, an interesting thing to proclaim to your wife and children at dinner.

Inside homophobia is misogyny: the act of being a man is a constant striving to not be a woman. If what a man does to a woman, or to anyone he penetrates, is imagined as violating and despoiling her, humiliation and degradation come to be indistinguishable from sexuality or a proxy for it in the puritanical imagination. So many of the thousands of sexual assault accounts I've read in recent years include acts that have nothing to do with the bodily satisfaction often presumed to be the goal. It's a version of love that's war, the enactment or realization of a set of metaphors in which men's bodies are weapons and women's bodies are targets, and queer bodies are hated for blurring the distinction or rejecting the metaphors.

Everyone is interdependent. Everyone is vulnerable. Everyone is penetrable, and everyone is penetrated incessantly by the vibrations of sound traveling into the inner ear, by the light shining in our eyes and on the surface of our bodies, by the air we must never stop breathing, by the food and water we take in, by the contacts that generate sensations that run from the surface of our skin to our brains, by the pheromones and bacteria we transmit imperceptibly to each other by air and contact, by the smells that are tiny particles we have inhaled, by the myriad species of beneficial bacteria in our gut and elsewhere that constitute so vast a portion of a human body that self is something of a misnomer or at least a crowd and maybe a party. If you were truly impenetrable you'd be dead in minutes, and there was a kind of deadening inertness that was part of the equation of imagining you could be so.

James Baldwin famously wrote, "If I am not what you say I am, then you are not who you think you are." Redefining women and their roles redefined men and masculinity and vice versa. If the genders were not opposite but a spectrum of variations on some central theme of being human, if there were many ways to execute your role or refuse it, and liberation for each gender was seen as being allowed to take up what had been considered the proper role and goods and even feelings of the other or find some third (or seventh) way, then the citadel would be broken and everyone could travel freely.

Heterosexual masculinity has often seemed to me a great renunciation, a repudiation not only of the myriad things that men are not supposed to like, but even a plethora of things that they are not supposed even to notice. Many of the gay men I knew noticed, and one of the pleasures of conversation with gay friends was an acute awareness of emotional, aesthetic, and political phenomena, an ability to weigh minute things and evaluate nuances and fine degrees of differentiation.

These men knew that words could be festive, recreational, medicinal, that banter and flirtation and extravagance, that humor and wryness and anecdotes of the absurd were pleasures worth pursuing. They knew that talk wasn't, as many straight men seemed to assume, just transactional, a way to dump or extract information or instructions. It could be play, riffing on ideas and tones; it could give encouragement and affection; and it could invite people to be themselves and to know themselves in order to be known. There were so many kinds of love at work: the love of vivid and exact description, which was sometimes poetic, sometimes skewering wit, sometimes deep insight, and of exchanges that wove connections between speakers and ideas.

If humor consists of noting the gap between what things are supposed to be and what they actually are—and much humor of the nonbrutal variety is—then those least invested in things as they are supposed to be, or who are actually adversaries and victims of conventionality, are most inclined and able to celebrate those gaps. The straight man is a figure in humor, the one who doesn't make or get the joke, and straight suggests linear thinking and conventional paths as well as heterosexuality.

I think of how for years when I encountered the great artist and graphic designer Rex Ray, who designed my first book, I'd shout "LambCHOP!!!" and he roared back in his rich, amused, rollicking voice, "CUPCAKE!!!" or of how when I was first getting to know the young architect Tim O'Toole around 1990, we'd greet each other with a caustic "HELLO, Kitty," bearing down on the first word, swinging back up with the second, so that the phrase was like a secret handshake, a badge of belonging. Of how I was free to be funny or dramatic or preposterous around them, and of how fun it was, and how much we laughed, and how there was room in there to be sad and bereft too. Even that could become something whose absurdities and excesses were occasion for more wit, because heartbreak and loneliness have their comic sides, and finding them can be key to survival. How it let me be someone I might not have gotten to be elsewhere. Not that all my gay friends were campy or even culture mavens. Bob Fulkerson was a rugged outdoorsman and political organizer, a fifth-generation Nevadan devoted to his state, but he was and is someone who calls me up sometimes just to leave me a message that he loves me, almost thirty years after we met at the Nevada Test Site.

Queer culture made it clear that a life can have as its stable foundation friendships so strong that they are a form of family, that family too can be liberated from the conventional roles of spousal contracts and begetting and blood kinship. It was a bulwark against the widespread, wearing insistence that only the nuclear family supplies love and stability—which sometimes it does, but we all know that sometimes it supplies misery and sabotage. This was, of course, in part the result of the exclusion of queer people from marriage and rejection by birth families long before marriage equality became the law of the land and adoptions became more available to same-sex couples. Later in life, when I forgot to tell interviewers that they would never ask a man that or to simply garrote them for being so noxious, I sometimes answered the intrusive questions about why I didn't marry and bear offspring with reference to being a San Franciscan, to being among people who had less conventional ideas of what a life could look like and what kinds of love could shore it up. It was a tremendous gift.

From that old apartment of mine I could walk west until I came to the Pacific Ocean. I could go almost due south to the Castro, where the theater and many other amenities and a shifting population of friends called me. I rarely walked north, though I drove there to cross the Golden Gate Bridge and plunge into the country—or to visit my mother, so that trips across the bridge meant both liberation and dread. It was an easy walk east to the Civic Center and to the main library, where I still do research, and to the trains to the East Bay. As the 1990s advanced, I spent more and more time driving across the Bay Bridge east to get to the American West, to the mountains and the deserts and the new life and friends I was finding there. Despite everything the world was opening up to me, or I to it.

Audibility, Credibility, Consequence

1

Growing up, we say, as though we were trees, as though altitude was all that there was to be gained, but so much of the process is growing whole as the fragments are gathered, the patterns found. Human infants are born with craniums made up of four plates that have not yet knit together into a solid dome so that their heads can compress to fit through the birth canal, so that the brain within can then expand. The seams of these plates are intricate, like fingers interlaced, like the meander of arctic rivers across tundra.

The skull quadruples in size in the first few years, and if the bones knit together too soon, they restrict the growth of the brain; and if they don't knit at all the brain remains unprotected. Open enough to grow and closed enough to hold together is what a life must also be. We collage ourselves into being, finding the pieces of a worldview and people to love and reasons to live and then integrate them into a whole, a life consistent with its beliefs and desires, at least if we're lucky.

The city was my great teacher in the 1980s, and that first book came out of what I learned from wandering streets and neighborhoods, from encountering subcultures and enclaves. The second came out of what the vast spaces of the mountains and deserts and the people there had to teach, and the lessons were magnificent, tremendous, sometimes terrifying, and the places brought new friends and a new sense of self.

At some point in my midtwenties, the childhood passion I had had for natural places had returned with a new intensity; I found epiphanies and a sense of liberty in being in the wild places—forests, grasslands, coastline—of my own region and began to study the cultural history of ideas and representations and desires for nature and place and landscape, first through art and art history, then through environmental literature and cultural histories, and then to write about it.

I began exploring and camping, wandering first in local places and English ideas of landscape and then into what lay over the horizon, the American West, the dry lands and open spaces that lay east of us, and non-Western ideas of nature that were more about understanding patterns and relationships than making pictures out of it all. (On those first camping trips, I was still so haunted by street violence that lying out in the open seemed reckless and terrifying; it took me a long time to get used to how rural safety consists of distance from danger, not the barriers against it and the recourse from it that urban structures and systems provide. I still don't camp alone, though I hike alone, generally with thoughts of danger not far away; access to nature is also contingent on your sense of safety, as people of color also know.) I steeped myself in images of and literature on landscape and began to focus on artists exploring ideas about place, landscape, nature, and travel.

The life I was looking for began taking root in the late 1980s. But it had many beginnings, as though I'd been planting many seeds, waiting and waiting while whatever secret germination and growth took place underground, before they burst into view. I began my first book, I made my first lasting friends, I found out how to go out into the larger world of the American West, I found, as they say, my voice.

I sometimes say that the Nevada Test Site taught me to write, because when I went there for the big spring antinuclear actions and campouts in 1988 and every year thereafter into the millennium, I met a place so stark and vast and, to me, strange, at which so many cultures and stories converged, that I had to bring together all the fragments of what I was doing into a new whole to have something that felt adequate to what I found there. Before then, I had accepted the pigeonholes into which writing fit. I had written criticism and reviews with a confident, objective-sounding tone, written journalistic reports that more or less colored within the lines of journalism. In those years, I had also written small, dense essays that were lyrical, personal, emotional, metaphorical, experimenting with form and tone, letting in what I was learning from poetry and the prophetic voice, doing all the things I was not supposed to do in criticism and journalism, letting wonder and melancholy and uncertainty in, giving rein to what language can do.

The Nevada Test Site was a place of convergence—of peoples, of histories, of values and ideas, of forces from the nuclear arms race to the Eurocentric reaction to deserts. To describe what it meant, I realized I needed all the modes of writing I'd learned and I needed them together, unsegregated. That was the major breakthrough of my writing, and *Savage Dreams*, the book that resulted, was the first exuberant experiment in bringing together the writing styles and voices and recognizing how they could be the same voice describing in terms historical, evocative, personal, analytical the complexity of a political situation and a historic moment.

It was a powerful place. I can feel what it was like to be there even now: the great expanses of dust-colored earth cobbled in stone, including shining pink quartz, fierce spiky plants here and there in the pale soil between stones, the dry air spectacularly clear (unless there was a dust storm or enough heat to make the air seethe and shimmer) so clear that you could see for dozens of miles to the fang-sharp ranges in the distance. Those immense spaces invited me to move freely and to feel the smallness of human bodies and concerns in a landscape where you could sometimes see a hundred miles, where you could drive half that without seeing a house, where you could, as I often did, wander toward the horizon feeling both liberated and fearful of what happens to a body that is two-thirds liquid in such an arid place. Just sitting still you could almost feel the water coming off your breath and out of your skin to disperse into the atmosphere where sometimes, rarely, in this driest part of the driest state in the union, clouds would gather and rain would evaporate as it fell or dash down only to dry up in minutes.

I had always been craving illimitable space. I found it earlier at Ocean Beach at the far end of the city and I found it as a child in the hills and sometimes lying on my back at night on the wild grass that reached down into the earth, looking into the stars until I felt that I could fall into them, found it in flying dreams, in wandering on foot, in wandering in time and space through books. And then I got more than I had dreamed of, almost as much as I needed.

It's generally recognized that you have to learn how to enter enclosed and guarded places, but to enter these vast spaces also takes application. A few years earlier, on a road trip with my boyfriend through Death Valley and the Southwest, we had turned back early, not knowing how to find the oases hidden in the valleys and canyons where water collects, or how to appraise the beauty that has little or no verdure, or how to let the quietness and sense of deep and cyclical time enter us. The Nevada Test Site was how I learned to enter, because these annual spring campouts and protests introduced me to people with deep ties to the remote places and gave me time and, quixotically, a place where I felt safe. Safe even though we were facing down the nuclear weapons being exploded not far away, wondering about the radioactive fallout we might be ingesting, and getting arrested, sometimes roughly, by the armed guards protecting the Test Site. Safe from assault because I was camping with friends among thousands of people dedicated to peace and disarmament (though dodging hippie dudes demanding hugs was an ongoing project for us young women).

My younger brother was instrumental in the Test Site organizing by the time he got me to come along in 1988, and it was a place where my environmentalism and his antiwar activism converged. The nuclear bombs being exploded there regularly were a brutality against all the living things downwind, reservation dwellers, ranchers, livestock, small-town people, and wildlife, in those rehearsals for the end-of-the-world war. Our family had immigrated to big cities and it sometimes seems to me that it was through those out-back adventures we had, with the ranchers, Native Nevadans, activists, Mormon downwinders, and atomic veterans we worked with and lived among, that the two of us finally truly arrived on the bare soil of this continent.

And then we became part of a great project to redefine it all. A number of Western Shoshone elders had joined us at the actions to say that the nuclear testing was being done on their land, which they'd like back, preferably without any more bombing and contamination. The environmental justice movement—an endeavor to address the race and class of who was impacted by environmental devastation—was gathering momentum and spreading new ways of thinking then. I had volunteered in the late 1980s at Earth Island Institute, an umbrella for a host of environmental projects, including a still-young Rainforest Action Network and EPOCA, the Environmental Project on Central America. Both addressed the fact that the tropical places they were trying to protect had long had human inhabitants and that human rights and environmental protection were inseparable goals. That may sound obvious now; it was new then.

It may be hard for those who came later to understand how utterly ignorant we non-Natives were then, how much Native people had disappeared from or never entered the mainstream conversation or were talked of exclusively in the past tense as people who had vanished long ago and would never appear to speak up on their own behalf. They were also treated as people who had never existed in the first place when artists, photographers, environmentalists, poets, explorers, historians imagined and depicted North America as a place in which human beings had just arrived, or rather that white men had recently discovered.

Ideas that seem ordinary now overthrew whole categories of thought then. They ended—to some extent, if not enough—an era of telling stories about a North American landscape that had been, until Europeans arrived, without human contact. I sometimes thought of this as the Madonna/whore theory of landscape: human contact was imagined as inevitably violating a vulnerable, passive nature that was inevitably degraded by us. White people were imagined as discoverers of a place that lay waiting, before history, before culture. Beyond this binary lay other ways of being human, other ways of being in the natural world. Being an environmentalist was coming to mean, at last, recognizing and respecting the first dwellers in these places and that human impact—hunting, harvesting, fire management techniques—had to be factored into assessments of what had constituted the ecosystems before Euro-American arrival. That is to say, these new frameworks and voices transformed nothing less than history, nature, and culture in far-reaching ways.

For me there was tremendous hope in the reemergence of people grounded in something other than the Judeo-Christian and European worldviews, who had lived in places for millennia without, for the most part, devastating them. The deep ties some had to the old ways and places seemed to me to provide crucial capacities to navigate the future (which I would see in full power with the Zapatistas of southern Mexico starting in 1994 and in the powerful presence of indigenous people in the twenty-first-century climate movement). The Native North American creation myths in which the world was never perfect, never fallen, and never finished being created shone a clear light on the problems with Genesis and the Judeo-Christian preoccupations with perfection and purity and the fall from grace. In those years I'd also been working with a Native California artist, Lewis DeSoto, whose installations and landscapes and ways of thinking about place and the sacred also showed me new perspectives and possibilities.

In 1990 I met environmental organizer Bob Fulkerson, a fifth-generation Nevadan, and he invited me to join some other Nevadans and journey farther into the state. It was on that short road trip that I grasped how extensive and destructive the military infrastructure was throughout the West, got a sense of these intrepid, resourceful, devoted Westerners dedicated to their rural and remote places along with a desire to join them and a sense that I had been looking for them since childhood. We stayed in touch, and Bob urged me to show up for the Western Shoshone sisters Mary and Carrie Dann's last day in court, in Reno, Nevada, in late spring of 1991. I did so. Their troubles had begun in 1973, when a federal agent asked Mary why she wasn't paying grazing fees on her cows. She told him that it wasn't federal land, and she was right that the treaty the Western Shoshone signed in 1863 did not cede their territory. The Danns pushed their claim all the way to the Supreme Court. They lost only because in the course of their case, the government invented a date that it had taken the land in the 1870s, a date that described no actual event, and decided it could compensate the tribe for the land in 1872 prices without interest. The traditionalists, catalyzed by the Danns, refused to accept the payment.

After the court case ended, Bob introduced me to Western Shoshone environmental organizer Virginia Sanchez, and she asked me to write an overarching history of Western Shoshone land rights for a small environmental publication. I took the assignment eagerly, and began it by spending several days in the archives of the University of Nevada in Reno. There I sat in a straight chair spooling through the microfilm of the CIA—the Commission on Indian Affairs that preceded the Bureau of Indian Affairs—reading, printing out, and taking notes on the reports of field officers in Nevada in the 1860s and 1870s. The reels of microfilm were scored with long horizontal scratches, and the letters were all written in beautiful copperplate handwriting that was hard to decipher, but what they meant became increasingly clear.

The neatness of the words unfurling in arcs and curves along hand-ruled pages suggested a kind of orderliness and propriety re-affirmed by the elaborate politeness in the salutations and the sign-offs in these letters about genocide. About how to push the Native people out of the way as whites flooded west and subjugate them and let their resources be pillaged, how to contain them and give them some handouts as their homelands were so degraded that food sources vanished. We would like the people involved in mon-strosity to be recognizably monstrous, but many of them are dili-gent, unquestioning, obedient adherents to the norms of their time, trained in what to feel and think and notice and what not to. The men who wrote these reports seemed like earnest bureaucrats, sometimes sympathetic to the plight of the people they were help-ing to exterminate, always convinced of their own decency. It is the innocence that constitutes the crime.

Somewhat relieved of mine, I became a member of the Western Shoshone Defense Project when it was created the next spring to support Mary and Carrie Dann as they prepared to face attack from the government. They were grand, fearless matriarchs, the most un-subjugated women I ever knew, queens of their household, heads of their ranch, capable of fixing a generator or taming a mustang from their vast herds, cheerful and pithy as they spoke to us in English and to each other in their own language. (*Savage Dreams*, my book in which they were principal figures, foregrounded a lot of charismatic women and women's groups, but I don't know if anyone recognized it as a feminist book.) To be around them was a revelation; it was to be where family memory reached back to before white people arrived, land was sacred, women were in charge, and actions should defend what mattered for the long future. I was getting an education about tangible things like the lay of the land and the history of the West, but also about matters of the spirit and questions of how to live your life.

Joining the project meant spending weeks at a time on the Danns' remote cattle ranch in northeastern Nevada, living out of my truck or an old trailer near their house, where I could plug in the desktop computer and printer I'd hauled out. It meant joining some friends from the antinuclear movement and some people I'd never met, indigenous and otherwise, as a coalition and attending tribal meetings and gatherings. It meant, in my case, ghostwriting letters and statements for Carrie and writing a lot of the literature for the project, press releases, and backgrounders (researching the long overview article I'd written after that immersion in the microfilm record had taught me a lot). And it meant waiting, because now that the courtroom conflict was over, the government was threatening to seize their livestock.

The violent assault came on April 11, 1992. An organizer at the ranch ran into a woman who asked him about all the sheriff's cars outside the community center in the nearest hamlet. The government had hired a roundup team to confiscate cattle, and law enforcement was there to back them up. I got the news by phone and within an hour had canceled all my plans and grabbed my stuff and headed east in my car, across the Bay Bridge, the East Bay, across the Sacramento River and the wide Sacramento Valley, up through the oak groves and then the pine groves and over the Sierra Nevada, and into the desert, dozed a couple of hours at a truck stop, and at dawn resumed driving the five hundred miles between my home and theirs. It was the first time I ever moved toward violence.

At ten in the morning, I found the heart of the ranch—the house, corrals, outbuildings, trailer—almost deserted. The conflict had happened elsewhere, on horseback, with the federal roundup team going after the livestock and the Shoshone supporters running interference on some of the Danns' tough saddle-broke mustangs. Carrie had argued about land rights and treaties with the federal agent and the local sheriff at the portable corral some of her cattle had been herded into, and the agent grabbed her arm to try to hinder her from intervening. She broke his grip and jumped into the corral and blocked the loading of the cattle. Unwilling to escalate, they went away. She won the battle, though the war dating back to the 1850s didn't end.

The struggle was never resolved, through difficulties, through conflicts within the tribe, through changing times, through the arrival of gold mines that scraped and developed and polluted their valley and pumped out its water and flooded the Dann family cemetery. I was sad about their stalemate and the government's war of attrition and grateful for my time with them. But the larger shift taking place made me hopeful as never before. I saw the power of people on the margins to change foundational stories, saw something absolutely unforeseen emerge, saw how, as those changes spread, signs and school textbooks, monuments, place names, land management practices, and sometimes laws changed, how museums gave back the bones and the relics to the people whose ancestors and treasures they were, how gradually all these tangible things meant something more important and less tangible.

It did not mean that everything was fine, but it was a profound shift with practical consequences, including in the understanding and management of natural systems and places. That transformation convinced me that culture could change politics, that representations could shape realities, that what we did as writers and historians mattered, that changing the story of the past could change the future. It was the genesis of a profound hope for me about the possibility of deep, unanticipated change and the capacity of those deemed marginal or insignificant to bring it about. The rising visibility and power of Native nations in the Americas felt of a piece with the nonviolent revolutions that had toppled the totalitarian regimes in Eastern Europe in 1989 and the dissolution of the Soviet Union a few years later, which I'd followed closely, with exhilaration.

That was my golden age, not because I had escaped the evils of this world but because I had found ways to think about them and sometimes do something about them, valiant companions in the efforts, places to fall in love with, and ideas that transformed me. I had begun returning to the place in which I spent the first two years of my life, Northern New Mexico, where I had the great fortune to be befriended by the older feminist writer Lucy Lippard, whose response to the manuscript of *Savage Dreams* was, essentially, to give me the key to her little house (and a nice blurb). I began spending part of every summer house-sitting for her out on the prairie, enraptured by the sky, the space, the light, and the thunderstorms. Later in the

1990s, I got involved with a man who lived in southeastern California's Mojave Desert and spent part of my time there for four years.

Our best as well as our worst emotions are contagious, and I benefited from the gallantry, boldness, dedication, and humor of all these Westerners close to the land (and Lucy's transplanted New England brisk fearlessness). And I grew close to the places themselves, and drew from them joys and strengths. I had developed the confidence to start moving freely around the West, gotten the pickup truck that let me go farther up dirt roads and into remote places and in whose camper shell I spent many nights, gotten friends in Utah, Colorado, New Mexico, and Nevada to visit. I was now roving across the western United States a lot, not to escape but to arrive in a deeper sense of home and to build and maintain ties across the region. I was cultivating a persona rooted in this place, in nonchalance about physical challenges ranging from driving and walking long distances to living outdoors and facing down the authorities in environmental protests. This was who I wanted to be, and some of it was a performance complete with trappings—pearl-snap shirts, dusty country-music cassette tapes for the pickup truck, a nice camp kit—but some of it went deeper.

The writing was going well enough that I felt hopeful about it and not so well that there were, as there would be later, a lot of demands on me. So I roamed and explored and made the most of the invitations that came my way. I was rich in time, and alive with excitement about the worlds and connections and ideas opening up to me. I miss the ability I had then to jump into my truck and go someplace for a week or two, to take the long way around, to linger and explore and not worry too much about obligations. I was free.

In the evenings when the sky near the horizon is apricot and the sky above is still blue I sometimes try to find the seam between the two colors, but in the heavens there is only a pallor between these opposites that is easy not to notice. Sometimes too in the evening I try to watch the colors change or a shadow grow longer across the landscape, and almost always my attention flickers for a moment and then I realize that the tree that was half in light has been swallowed by darkness or the brightness and sharp shadows have suddenly diffused because the sun has dipped or the sky that was cobalt is now midnight blue. Things are one way and then another and the transitions are hard to mark.

The present becomes the past through increments too small to measure; suddenly something that is becomes something that was, and the way we live is not the way we lived. So much of what changed is hard for those who lived through it to remember and those who came after to imagine. In many parts of American society, kindness has increasingly become a criterion applied to all forms of interaction, but its absence before was elusive, because it's too easy to not notice who and what is not in the room. Myriad forms of injustice became visible in ways that made it seem normal to recognize them and easy to forget by what toil they became visible (which always raises the question of what else we do not yet see, and for what failings future eras will rebuke us). The evolution of feminism makes some of the formerly nameless unrecognizability of many kinds of discrimination hard to recall, though that is one measure of the difference between then and now.

There were epic public changes that make the era of my youth a foreign country, one in which I no longer live and which the young will never visit, and most will never know how different it was and why it changed and who to thank. My own life metamorphosed by degrees I would only perceive in retrospect. I was almost friendless, and the friends I had made as a teenager and in my early twenties were mostly bad fits; perhaps it was because I didn't know who I was or wanted to be someone else and so I didn't know who was like me or who liked me. Or because kindness was not a criterion. Then later in my twenties I made friends who have lasted, and then some more, and then that sense of being on the far edge alone became a sense of being on the borderlands between various realms, so that I began to have the pleasure of bringing ideas, projects, and people from one circle to another, and the lack and loneliness were gone.

I went through a phase of approaching the powers that I had assumed were not for me and maybe not for my gender. I bought a motorcycle at the beginning of the 1990s, and revving the engine and kick-starting it and moving its weight to park it or bring it back upright or pick it up when it got knocked over gave me a kind of macho pleasure (more than riding it, which I always found a little scary, because of cars, before it was stolen nine months after I bought it). I learned to work out with weights and weight machines shortly thereafter, having finally noticed that the body requires maintenance and that the stress that petrified my form yielded at least temporarily to violent exertion.

Two or three years later, the boyfriend who lived in the Mojave taught me to shoot a .22 rifle—we went out into the desert and aimed at Old English malt liquor cans late one beautiful afternoon until evening came and our shadows stretched for a hundred feet and more across the flat ground. I found it alarmingly fun, though when we went shooting with his father, who'd spent his life in the military and a lot of time in combat, he told me the story of being forced by a general's direct orders to shoot a civilian on a hill a long way away—and how he had nightmares ever after. It was a solemn and graceful warning to take guns seriously. And I studied Shoto-kan karate for a little while with a world champion fighter who feared nothing when she walked down the street. Just to shout and kick and strike required a different sense of self. Each of these felt like a little usurpation of powers that I had once believed were not for people like me. Things were changing.

Street harassment largely ceased to be a problem, and my wariness softened, though it never went away. It was not a science experiment with a control, so it's hard to say what exactly changed. Perhaps I aged out of my prime target years. Perhaps the culture changed in some way, though I know young women still suffer street harassment and assault. Perhaps the ways I became street-smart were a factor: I learned how to give those I encountered respect and acknowledgment, and to not get caught up in anyone else's drama—to be fluid on the street, moving smoothly without snagging or rushing. White men fell silent. The commentary from the black men in my neighborhood grew uniformly cordial, as some of it always had been, and I tried to say pleasant things back, and enjoyed the interactions.

I published short pieces and reviews and then longer pieces and more ambitious essays. I wrote a book and then a more ambitious book and then another in that vein and then I wrote my history of walking, *Wanderlust*, which appeared in 2000, the first book for which I got an advance that approximated a living wage, the first book that circulated widely. Each book answered a question I began with and by its end generated other questions. That history of walking made me wonder about two things that I explored in what became my next two books.

I wrote *A Field Guide to Getting Lost* to go deeper into ideas about wandering, venturing into the unknown, coming to terms with the essential mystery at the heart of things, and about loss. I was not sure whether I would ever show it to anyone, or whether I would finish it or whether it was publishable, or whether I wanted to publish it. Then I did and it had a quiet life at first and then an interesting one as people found it and quoted it and some artists made work in response to it.

The other of the two books to emerge from *Wanderlust* was about technological change and the disembodiment that came with the transcendence of time and space that machines made possible, and it was centered on Eadweard Muybridge, the British photographer who laid the groundwork for what became motion pictures (and documented San Francisco, where he lived during much of his prime, when he murdered his wife's lover, made some of the greatest landscape and panoramic photographs of the nineteenth century, and transformed, with high-speed sequential photography, what scientists and artists knew about humans in motion).

Something else shifted in the work around the time the Muybridge book was published in the spring of 2003. It came in part from seeing Barry Lopez and Terry Tempest Williams talk and from meeting Susan Sontag. I asked myself why, though I was writing about politics in various ways, I wasn't speaking as directly as Sontag was to what was in the news, or as Barry and Terry were to what lay underneath the news, the terrors and yearnings and ideals that drive our public as well as our private selves. And I was beginning to collect stories that illustrated my evolving sense of how the world gets changed and where power lies and what the case for hope is.

Another one of my amusingly awful encounters with older white men helped bring together that collection of ideas into the May 2003 essay "Hope in the Dark" and the 2004 book of that title. One day in the spring of 2003, my work was featured in a university colloquium with a man who launched an extended ad hominem attack on me, my motives, and my hopefulness. I'd arrived at that hopefulness in the course of pursuing a return project in Yosemite National Park. In 2001, with the artists Mark Klett and Byron Wolfe, I'd ventured in to rephotograph Eadweard Muybridge's photographs there and understand what had changed since he made them in 1872. Our project grew into a broader survey of earlier photographers, modernist as well as Victorian, and of what had and had not changed since their times. The exploration gave me a magnificently complex sense of change as something that does not occur at a predictable rate but varies widely from place to place and entity to entity: some trees were still recognizable more than a century later, some arrangements of small boulders had not moved in all that time, but the Merced River had shifted its bed, forests had devoured meadows, and celebrated old landmarks had vanished.

I thought I was there to look at change over the span of 130 years, but I was astonished to find how much had changed in less than a decade since I had scrutinized the place for *Savage Dreams*. Native people had gained some rights and a lot more representation in the park. Before whites had arrived, they had set fires as part of their land management techniques, and the Park Service had finally recognized fire as part of the place's ecology after a century of fire suppression. And the park's visitors were far more ethnically diverse; the sense of one cosmology having been pushed out by another was giving way, or so it seemed to me, to a sense of the coexistence of many worldviews and a big adjustment in the Eurocentric one to recognize—imperfectly, incompletely, but still—the rights and presence of indigenous Americans. California was on its way to becoming a nonwhite-majority state and some of the promise of that I had found in the park this time around.

This was the hopeful vision I'd presented at the university, where the academic man had laid into my motives and my character for half an hour or so, in front of the students I'd brought from the writing class I was teaching at an art school. He was attached to his narratives that everything was getting worse, to his despair (and, I was told by mutual friends, resentful that my pile of publications kept growing). I was appalled I'd brought these young women, at my dean's urging, to hear elevated discourse and they'd heard this instead. The whole thing churned in my head until a couple of days later when I got up before dawn and returned to that old desk in the east bay window of my home and wrote until sunrise arrived and a raven landed on the telephone wires just beyond the window and I'd made the preliminary case for hope to my satisfaction. "Thank you for sitting all the way through my, um, very interesting colloquium, and a special thanks to Maggie and Kristina for making supportive faces at me from across the room," I wrote them. "For me, the ultimate subject is what kinds of histories can we imagine and can we tell."

The academic conflict over my ideas had taken place thirteen days before the Iraq War began in a hail of American bombs on March 20, 2003. Earlier that year I'd put together a group of my friends—a Gulf War vet, a singer who was an old friend from the Nevada Test Site days, a gay Cuban Buddhist, an astrophysicist, a domestic violence advocate—under the rubric B.A.D.A.S.S., the Bay Area Direct Action Secret Society. We were part of a global movement that the month before had held the biggest demonstration in world history, in thousands of locations, hundreds of countries, on all seven continents. We dressed as superheroes, dressed in business casual, dressed in white with our own faces in white masks and the faces of Iraqi children on our chests, dressed in black. We marched, we did street theater, we sang, and then the bombs began falling and, horrorstruck, we helped shut down the city's financial district.

Many years later I heard a story from Natashia Deón who was then a corporate attorney living in a high-rise near that district. On one of the big days of protest, she came down from her perch to buy a soda, looked around at the throngs on the boulevard, and wondered what she was doing with her life. She decided to change it. She became a lawyer who defends the indigent, passionately, and then, a few years after we became friends, a successful novelist.

What she told me years later was the kind of story I'd collected to make the case that you can't assume that you know why what you're doing matters. You can't at least declare failure immediately, because consequences are not always direct, or immediate, or obvious, and the indirect consequences matter.

When the bombing of Baghdad began, some of the friends I'd protested with and others around me extrapolated from the fact that they had not stopped the war the idea that they had not achieved anything, and sometimes they traveled onward from there to the idea they'd never achieved anything, had no power, and that we were all doomed. Despair became a machine that would grind up anything you fed it. That prompted me to work harder on the case for hope I was building. I'd been informally collecting passages and examples, and on the day after the attack at the university forum I'd written that letter making the case for hope to send to some of the people who'd been in attendance there. Disagreement often prompts clarification, at least in my case, and it can be useful even when its intention is adversarial. Half my muses have been haters.

After the war began, I worked in a sort of trance all day and into the night for three or four days to shape the material into the essay "Hope in the Dark." Anecdotes and examples that had been accruing for years suddenly had a pattern to fit into, and the pattern was the case for hope. Some of it was recycled from the letter to my students. It was the first thing I published exclusively online, and it went viral as nothing I'd ever done before had, picked up by alternative weeklies, reprinted as a small booklet by a graphic designer, forwarded over and over by email in those days before social media.

I argued that we had a lot of power, a history of forgotten and undervalued victories, that while some things were getting worse, the long view—especially if you were nonmale, or nonstraight, or nonwhite—showed some remarkable improvement in our rights and roles, and that the consequences of our acts were not knowable in advance. They were often not knowable soon afterward and sometimes ever after since great strategists, idealists, and movements sometimes prompt indirect repercussions in other times and places and struggles. I'd seen nonviolent direct action liberate Eastern European countries from their totalitarian governments in 1989, seen the Zapatista insurgency emerge from the Lacandon jungle in 1994, seen the government of Canada create the vast indigenous-governed territory of Nunavut in 1999, seen things I'd never dreamed possible come to pass. In 2004 I turned the essay on hope into a small book, and over the following years it came out in a dozen other countries and languages.

My university interlocutor had accused me of offering palliatives for marketing reasons, but what I'd wanted to offer is encouragement, a word that, though it carries the stigma of niceness, literally means to instill courage. Encouragement not to make people feel good, but to make them feel powerful. I'd eventually realize that what I was doing could equally be characterized as stealing away the best excuse for doing nothing: that you have no power and nothing you do matters. It was nurture of people's sense of possibility, and it was dissent from a lot of the most familiar narratives in which despair and cynicism—that weird formula in which overconfidence about outcome undermines one's will to play a role—justify nonparticipation. Something profound had shifted for me to feel capable of changing minds and responsible for tending to hearts. A sense of powerlessness and disconnectedness had faded away and a sense of possibility had replaced it, about my own capacity and role as well as about the way that change itself works.

Over the next several years, I became a political writer, writing essays in response to unfolding events and chronic situations and circulating them via a website that got picked up by news sites all over the world. It was often the worst things, the things I disagreed with or was outraged by, that inspired me to write, though I wrote a lot about what I loved as well—and what I opposed I opposed because it harmed or threatened to harm what I loved. And then I wrote something that took on a wild life of its own, wrote it as casually as I'd ever written anything. Everything else I ever wrote was on a subject I chose and approached intentionally, but feminism chose me or was something I couldn't stay away from.

3

In those days I often headed my emails to Tina with weather reports, since she had moved far away for a teaching position and missed the Bay Area. We had been writing almost daily for years, and sometimes multiple times a day. On March 24, 2008, we'd been continuing the back-and-forth on an email from March 20 that I'd headed FULL MOON, EQUINOX, PRETTY DAY BUT CHILLY. That evening of March 24 I'd written her with a new heading, LONG FAINT HERRINGBONE CLOUDS BEFORE DUSK.

Two years before, I had left the studio apartment for a more spacious attic dwelling six blocks south. My friend Marina had just moved in with me there, in flight from an awful soon-to-be-ex, and I was delighted to have her with me. By the time of the alarming diagnosis I'd received that winter, we were close friends. The diagnosis meant major surgery a few weeks before this time, so we were nestled in, convalescing, each in our own way. She was one of those people with whom a conversation once opened up tumbles and flows of its own accord, with jokes and laughter mixed in with explorations of ideas and events, aspirations and emotions, the conversations I'd dreamed of.

A friend to talk to in person, a friend to write to every day. It was a hard time, and there is grumbling in the email to Tina, but I had reached a point where my social life was all that I could desire. Marina, who usually had a birdlike brightness of eye, a vivacity and an exceptional emotional warmth, as well as a brilliant political mind, had been subdued after her separation until that evening of the long faint herringbone clouds. Thanks to the email (Tina also liked food descriptions), I know I'd made us a dinner of pasta, artichokes, and greens from the Civic Center Farmers' Market, and that I had invited over my younger brother, also a close friend of hers, who joined us after he had participated in a demonstration in which 4,000 candles were lit for victims of a massacre, and that we had drunk a bottle of red wine, and under that mild influence Marina had recovered her sparkle and her verve.

The herringbone clouds letter didn't mention that I had been joking that night, as I had for years, about writing an essay called "Men Explain Things to Me." I'd brought it up at the dinner on my little drop-leaf oak dining table with the massive vaselike center legs, the one I'd bought from the elderly lesbian couple next door. When I did, Marina had energetically urged me to write the piece and said how much young women like her sister needed it.

Many years later, in the apartment I currently inhabit, I sat at another kitchen table, with a film actress who had come to talk with me about feminism. The next day an enormous bouquet arrived with a card quoting back what she liked best of what I had said: "It's not you, it's patriarchy," which might be one of feminism's basic messages. That is, there's nothing wrong with you; there's something wrong with the system that bears down on you and tells you you're useless, incompetent, untrustworthy, worthless, wrong. Marina heard in my anecdotes the possibility of telling that to the world or to some women in it, and she thought they ought to hear it.

I was an early riser, and she was catching up on much-needed sleep, and the attic had just two large rooms. The kitchen and the daybed on which guests slept were in the west room. The east room was my bedroom and office, with a long, built-in desktop held up at its center by the old spindle-legged desk. So the morning of the 25th, rather than disturb her rest, I sat down at that desk once again and did her bidding. The essay poured out with ease or rather tumbled out seemingly of its own accord. When this happens it means that the thoughts have long been gestating and writing is only a birth of what was already taking form out of sight. So much of the work of writing happens when you are seemingly not working, made by that part of yourself you may not know and do not control, and when the work shows up like that your job is to get out of its way.

What I wrote that morning startled me, because when I had been joking the night before, I hadn't connected men explaining things to me to what I would write that morning. The essay's beginning is comedy: in an incident from five years earlier, a man talks over me to explain my own book to me and is briefly stunned to realize (when my companion finally succeeds in interrupting him) that I, the person he's already dismissed and turned into an audience, am the author of that "very important book" on Muybridge on which he is holding forth.

I've sometimes been taken to task by people as though I equate minor indignities with major crimes, people who don't or prefer not to understand that we talk about a lot of things on a spectrum, and we can distinguish the different points on the spectrum, but the point is that it's one spectrum. Making black people drink out of separate drinking fountains and lynching them are different in degree and kind, but they both emerge from the same effort to enforce segregation and inequality, and almost no one has trouble understanding that.

Since the essay I wrote that morning was published, I've heard from lawyers, scientists, doctors, scholars in many fields, athletes and mountaineers, mechanics, builders, film technicians, and other women who've had their field of expertise explained to them by men who didn't have any idea what they were talking about but thought the world was so ordered that knowledge was inherent in them as lack of it was in women, that listening was our natural state and obligation and holding forth their right, perhaps that it is her job to let his sense of self expand as hers shrivels. That asymmetry about who's in charge of the facts applied to everything from intellectual matters to what just happened a moment ago, and it undermines women's capacity to do almost anything, including, sometimes, survive.

The essay begins with that funny anecdote about the man who told me about the very important Muybridge book. The essay's next anecdote from my own life was something else:

When I was very young and just beginning to get what feminism was about and why it was necessary, I had a boyfriend whose uncle was a nuclear physicist. One Christmas, he was telling—as though it were a light and amusing subject—how a neighbor's wife in his suburban bomb-making community had come running out of her house naked in the middle of the night screaming that her husband was trying to kill her. How, I asked, did you know that he wasn't trying to kill her? He explained, patiently, that they were respectable middle-class people. Therefore, her-husband-trying-to-kill-her was simply not a credible explanation for her fleeing the house yelling that her husband was trying to kill her. That she was crazy, on the other hand. . . .

The same assumption that you are incompetent in your field of expertise may mean you're viewed as incompetent to know if someone is trying to kill you. It's an assumption that has resulted in death for many victims of domestic violence and stalking. This essay headed to places I did not know I was going to go.

I am a woman who when a poet friend spoke to me of an incident with a nun in Catholic school as "the only time anyone ever hit me" was staggered to try to imagine a life as safe and calm as hers in this respect. I am the daughter of a man who considered it his right to hit women and children and did as his father did before him, and of a woman who had or felt she had for two decades no recourse from that man and no place to register a complaint. I am a woman who by the first years of my teens had to learn to squirm and worm and fade away when adult men pursued me because telling them to leave me alone was in that era of my youth inconceivable as something I had the right or even the safety to say and they had the obligation or even inclination to heed. I am a woman who during my youth thought it likely I would be raped and maybe also murdered and all my life have lived in a world where women were raped and murdered by strangers for being women and by men they knew for asserting their rights or just being women and where those rapes and murders were lasciviously lingered on in art. I am a woman who has been told at crucial times that I was not believable and that I was confused and that I was not competent to deal in facts. And in all that I am ordinary. After all, I live in a society where rape kits and campus stalking awareness month and domestic violence shelters in which women and children are supposed to hide from husbands and fathers are normal fixtures.

And I am a woman who became a writer and through it gained some standing while writing about other things from art to war, and sometimes tried to put that standing to work to try to open up space for others' voices. I am a woman who one morning wrote an essay called "Men Explain Things to Me" that is about the way that the mild disparagement of having your subject of expertise explained to you by a fool who does not know that he does not know what he's talking about or who he's talking to is on a spectrum, and that the other end of the spectrum is full of violent death.

I had a version of the essay printed out to put on the breakfast table with Marina's coffee and my tea a couple of hours later, and at 10:42 that morning I sent thirteen friends, including Tina, the essay in an email also titled MEN EXPLAIN THINGS TO ME. That morning's version had a little superfluous ornamentation weeded out before publication, including, to my surprise when I look now, an epigraph from Keats's "Ode to a Nightingale," but it is very close to the essay I published online and, in truncated version, in the *Los Angeles Times* a few weeks later.

I had written about my own experiences and perceptions, and they had turned out to have a lot in common with other women's experiences and perceptions. It went viral immediately and got millions of hits at the website Guernica over the years because the experiences and situations I described were so brutally common and so inadequately acknowledged. It has most likely had more impact than anything else I've done, this essay I wrote in one sitting that morning. As the title essay of a 2014 anthology of my feminist essays, it became a bestseller in South Korea and stayed that way for years in the United States, and it appeared in several other languages from Danish to Spanish to Farsi.

It prompted an anonymous commenter at the website LiveJournal to coin the word *mansplaining* soon after it first appeared, a word that caught on, that entered the *Oxford English Dictionary* in 2014, that is now widely known and used in English, exists in dozens of languages, and has begat a host of variations such as *whitesplaining* (and that's often credited to me, though I did not coin it). It also provided some encouragement I'm proud of. A very famous woman writer, soon after the essay appeared, sent it to a well-known pundit, a bellicose misogynist, with this message: "Reading this wonderful essay by Rebecca Solnit reminded me of something I have been meaning to say to you for a long, long time. Go fuck yourself," and it prompted one young woman I met to get divorced.

I have been thrilled and moved by the young women who came up to me to say that something I've written helped them locate their power and their value and reject their subjugation. You don't really know what you do when you write, because it depends on how people read, and there are ways that knowing their appetites and interests can guide you down familiar paths and ways that not knowing can take you to appetites and interests you didn't know existed and sometimes your readers didn't either. There's a Buddhist phrase about the work of bodhisattvas: "the liberation of all beings." I see feminism as a subset of that work.

4

A writer's voice is supposed to be hers alone. It's what makes someone distinct and recognizable, and it's not quite style and not just tone or subject; it's something of the personality and the principles of the writer, where your humor and seriousness are located, what you believe in, why you write, who and what you write about, and who you write for. But the feminist themes that became a major part of my work after "Men Explain Things to Me" is for and about and often with the voices of other women talking about survival.

That work of mine sometimes included a chorus and sometimes joined one. When you pursue creative work, immortality is often held up as an ideal. You're supposed to aspire to make something that will be recognized and that will, as they say, "keep your name alive," and it's true that words are alive when they're read or heard. But I learned from the artists I researched and wrote about and the movements that changed the culture that there are two ways of making contributions that matter. One is to make work that stays visible before people's eyes; the other is to make work that is so deeply absorbed that it ceases to be what people see and becomes how they see. It is no longer in front of them; it's inside them. It is no longer the artist; it's the people who are no longer only the audience.

Works of art that had an impact in their time sometimes look dated or obvious because what was fresh and even insurrectionary about them has become the ordinary way things are, how we edit films or see history or nature or sexuality or understand rights and their violations. Thus the vision of one or of a few becomes the perspective of many. They have been rendered obsolete by their success—which makes the relevance of even much nineteenth-century feminist writing a grim reminder that though we've come far, it's not far enough.

I've sometimes thought immortality is a desert idea, from the monotheistic fanaticisms of the desert, where a scar or a treasure can last for thousands of years, where some Bedouin shepherds can take the Dead Sea Scrolls out of a jar in a cave about twenty-two hundred years after they were put there—including the Book of Isaiah reminding us that "all flesh is grass." In humid places everything decays, and much decays back into the soil, and that soil nurtures new life, and perhaps the best thing creative work can do is to compost into the soil so that, unremembered, it becomes the food of a new era, or rather, devoured, digested, the very consciousness of that era. Marble lasts, but soil feeds.

My life has spanned a revolution against the old authoritarianisms. In response to the late 1950s and early 1960s crises of nuclear fallout and pesticides, ordinary people questioned the authority of the scientists in service of the military and the chemical companies, and then the nascent environmental movement asked broader questions about anthropocentrism, capitalism, consumerism, and ideas of progress and the domination of nature. Racial justice movements questioned the centrality of whiteness, gay and lesbian liberation movements questioned the centrality of heterosexuality, and feminism questioned patriarchy (and when we were lucky, these boulevards intersected). Though they were more than questions; they were demands for change and for the redistribution of power and value.

Change is the measure of time, and these movements were often regarded as having failed to realize short-term or specific goals, but in the long term they often changed the very premises by which decisions were made and facts were interpreted, and how people imagined themselves, each other, their possibilities, their rights, and society. And who decided, who interpreted, what was visible and audible, whose voice and vision mattered.

Feminism was in a lull in 2008, when I wrote that essay. Many things progress the way feminism has in recent years, with an unpredictable pattern of gradual change, or stagnation, or regression, punctuated by sudden crises in which the situation and collective imagination change rapidly. For feminism these eruptions have often been around a dramatic event in the news. In 2012 campus antirape activists in the USA were becoming more visible and audible and effective, and then two crimes got a lot of media coverage—the Steubenville, Ohio, gang sexual assault on an incapacitated sixteen-year-old in August and the New Delhi rape-disembowelment-murder of Jhoti Singh on a public bus that December—and something changed.

Or something had already changed, because these were ordinary horrible stories that got an extraordinary amount of coverage, perhaps because who decides what is news and from whose perspective it will be told had already changed. For what seemed to me the first time, these stories were presented as emblematic of an epidemic rather than, as such crimes almost always had been before, as isolated anomalous incidents that didn't raise questions about how common such violence is and how it affects women in general. When the long tolerated is suddenly seen as intolerable, someone has become audible and someone else has begun listening for the first time.

At the beginning of 2013 a dam broke. Behind it were millions of women's stories about sexual violence, violence made possible by their inaudibility and lack of credibility and the inconsequentiality of their stories. Torrents of stories poured forth. In response to the misogyny-driven Isla Vista massacre of 2014 by a young man who hated women and wanted to punish them for not delivering the sex he thought he was entitled to. In response to a sports star beating his fiancée, in response to women being discredited and attacked for speaking up about a celebrity who'd assaulted them. In response to the 2017 revelations about sexual abuse first in the film industry and then in every industry from the restaurant business to the agricultural fields and the tech industry in the upheaval called #MeToo, and then beyond the USA, from Iceland to South Korea. In response to the 2018 Supreme Court hearing at which a woman told her story of being assaulted at age fifteen, and the residual trauma, and received death threats as a result of speaking up.

The brutality of what we examined and the exhilaration at being able to tell and at the power of telling made an odd mix, and the storytellers were both liberated and returned to their suffering as they spoke. Through each rupture poured so many stories that it seemed as though everything hidden had come out into the open, and then another rupture happened, and thousands or hundreds of thousands more women told their stories for the first time.

Violence against bodies had been made possible on an epic epidemic scale by violence against voices. The existing order rested on the right and capacity of men to be in charge—of meaning and of truth, of which stories mattered and whose got told, as well as of more tangible phenomena (money, law, government, media) that maintained the arrangement. And it rested on the silence or silencing of those whose experiences demonstrated the illegitimacies of the status quo and those atop it. But something essential had changed. The change was often seen as a beginning but I saw it as a culmination of the long, slow business of making feminist perspectives more widespread and putting more women (and men who regarded women as equal and credible) in positions of power as editors, producers, directors, journalists, judges, heads of organizations, senators.

The rise of social media and the plethora of new online forums created space for many more voices, and these amplified individual stories brought their own testimony to the conversation, and fortified the diagnosis and the need for change. This chorus created a broad river whose current carried individual voices such as mine; to the extent that the world has been changed, it was a collective project carried out by many millions.

It's often assumed that anger drives such work, but most activism is driven by love, a life among activists has convinced me. Too, though the remedies for trauma most often proffered in our privatized society are personal, doing something for and with others, something to change the circumstances under which you were harmed, is often an experience of connection and power that overcomes that sense of isolation and powerlessness central to trauma.

Writing about sexual assault and misogyny has been the easiest writing I've ever done, perhaps because what drives me is a force harder to stop than to start. It requires a deep immersion in hideous crimes; for many years, over and over, I have read about rape at breakfast and beatings and stalkings at lunch and had murder for dinner, taken in many thousands of such stories, and yet because all this is coming to light in a new way, and because there is some possibility of transforming the situations and shifting the power, this ferocious drive overwhelms the horror and the terror and is perhaps the first thing that has.

At the Nevada Test Site I learned that you deal with the worst things by facing them directly. If you run away from them, they chase you; if you ignore them, they catch you unprepared; and it's in facing them that you find allies and powers and the possibility of winning. So it was that I tried several times before to face and name gender violence in my writing and eventually found what I had so long waited for, a global movement of women facing it and creating the conversation we needed.

Storytelling was our central tool. We pointed out how often the same tropes, clichés, and excuses are used, the same assumptions are made, the same people are protected and believed, the same people are discredited and punished. We stripped away the old excuses, the victim blaming and trivializing, by making the patterns obvious, by insisting, for example, that rapists cause rape and not alcohol, outfits, or the desire of women to go places and talk to people. Finally, we talked about stalking, harassment, assault, rape, domestic violence, and femicide as different manifestations of the same misogyny. The conversation about feminism broadened and deepened knowledge of how sexual abuse takes place, why victims often don't report it and seldom lie but are often disbelieved when they do report, why perpetrators are rarely convicted. The ways that race and gender intersect were one of the things that came into focus in new ways, and so did the analogies between the two as the ways that racial violence also are licensed by devaluing, discrediting, blaming, or ignoring the victims.

5

It took me ten years and dozens of feminist essays from that morning I wrote "Men Explain Things to Me" to realize that I was not talking and writing, after all, about violence against women, though I was reading about it incessantly. I was writing about what it means not to have a voice and making the case for a redistribution of that vital power. The crucial sentence in "Men Explain Things to Me" is "Credibility is a basic survival tool." But I was wrong that it's a tool. You hold a tool in your own hands, and you use it yourself. What it does is up to you.

Your credibility arises in part from how your society perceives people like you, and we have seen over and over again that no matter how credible some women are by supposedly objective standards reinforced by evidence and witnesses and well-documented patterns, they will not be believed by people committed to protecting men and their privileges. The very definition of women under patriarchy is designed to justify inequality, including inequality of credibility.

Though patriarchy often claims a monopoly on rationality and reason, those committed to it will discount the most verifiable, coherent, ordinary story told by a woman and accept any fantastical account by a man, will pretend sexual violence is rare and false accusations common, and so forth. Why tell stories if they will only bring forth a new round of punishment or disparagement? Or if they will be ignored as if they meant nothing? This is how preemptive silencing works.

To have a voice means not just the animal capacity to utter sounds but the ability to participate fully in the conversations that shape your society, your relations to others, and your own life. There are three key things that matter in having a voice: audibility, credibility, and consequence.

Audibility means that you can be heard, that you have not been pressed into silence or kept out of the arenas in which you can speak or write (or denied the education to do so—or, in the age of social media, harassed and threatened and driven off the platform, as so many have).

Credibility means that when you get into those arenas, people are willing to believe you, by which I don't mean that women never lie, but that stories should be measured on their own terms and context, rather than patriarchy's insistence that women are categorically unqualified to speak, emotional rather than rational, vindictive, incoherent, delusional, manipulative, unfit to be heeded—those things often shouted over a woman in the process of saying something challenging (though now death threats are used as a shortcut, and some of those threats are carried out, notably with women who leave their abusers, because silencing can be conversational or it can be premeditated murder).

To be a person of consequence is to matter. If you matter, you have rights, and your words serve those rights and give you the power to bear witness, make agreements, set boundaries. If you have consequence, your words possess the authority to determine what does and does not happen to you, the power that underlies the concept of consent as part of equality and self-determination.

Even legally women's words have lacked consequence: in only a few scattered places on earth could women vote before the twentieth century, and not so many decades ago, women rarely became lawyers and judges; I met a Texas woman whose mother was among the first women in their region to serve on a jury, and I was an adult when the first woman was appointed to the U.S. Supreme Court. Until a few decades ago, wives throughout much of the world, including the United States, lacked the right to make contracts and financial decisions or even to exercise jurisdiction over their own bodies that overrode their husbands' ability to do so; in some parts of the world, a wife is still property under the law, and others choose her husband. To be a person of no consequence, to speak without power, is a bewilderingly awful condition, as though you were a ghost, a beast, as though words died in your mouth, as though sound no longer traveled. It is almost worse to say something and have it not matter than to be silent.

Women have been injured on all three fronts—as have men of color and nonwhite women doubly so. Not allowed to speak or punished for speaking or excluded from the arenas—courts, universities, legislatures, newsrooms—where decisions are made. Mocked or disbelieved or threatened if they do find a place in which to speak, and routinely categorized as inherently deceitful, spiteful, delusional, confused, or just unqualified. Or they speak up and it is no different than remaining silent; they have told their stories and nothing happens, because their rights and their capacity to bear witness don't matter, so their voices are just sounds that blow away on the wind.

Gender violence is made possible by this lack of audibility, credibility, and consequence. We live inside an enormous contradiction: a society that by law and preening self-regard insists it is against such violence has by innumerable strategies allowed that violence to continue unchecked; better and far more frequently protected perpetrators than victims; and routinely punished, humiliated, and intimidated victims for speaking up, from workplace harassment cases to campus rape cases to domestic violence cases. The result makes crimes invisible and victims inaudible people of no consequence.

The disregard for a woman's voice that underlies sexual violence is inseparable from the disregard afterward if a woman goes to the police, the university authorities, her family, her church, the courts, to the hospital for a rape kit, and is ignored, discredited, blamed, shamed, disbelieved. They are both assaults on the full humanity and membership of a person in her society, and the devaluation in the latter arena enables the former. Sexual assault can only thrive in situations of unequal audibility, credibility, and consequence. This, far more than any other disparity, is the precondition for epidemic gender violence.

Changing who has a voice with all its power and attributes doesn't fix everything, but it changes the rules, notably the rules about what stories will be told and heard and who decides. One of the measures of this change is the many cases that were ignored, disbelieved, dismissed, or found in favor of the perpetrator years ago that have had a different outcome in the present, because the women or children who testified have more audibility, credibility, and consequence now than they did before. The impact of this epochal shift that will be hardest to measure will be all the crimes that won't happen because the rules have changed.

Behind that change are transformations in whose rights matter and whose voice will be heard and who decides. Amplifying and reinforcing those voices and furthering that change was one of the tasks to which I put the voice I'd gained as a writer, and seeing that what I and others wrote and said was helping to change the world was satisfying in many ways to me as a writer and as a survivor.

Afterword:
Lifelines

One day in New Orleans in late 2013 I was sitting behind a table in a narrow room signing books for a long line of people, along with my coeditor, native New Orleanian Rebecca Snedeker, when a woman took my hand in hers and began to read my palm. The book was our atlas of that city, my fifteenth or sixteenth or seventeenth book, depending on how you count them. I'd come to New Orleans six months after Hurricane Katrina, on Easter weekend of 2006, and been drawn into the untold stories of the storm and its aftermath, gotten involved in trying to expose some of the racial crimes, which I prodded investigative journalists to look at and wrote about myself in my 2009 book about disasters and the remarkable societies that arise in the wreckage, *A Paradise Built in Hell*.

I'd shown up in New Orleans to look at what was ugliest about the city: poverty and racism and how more than 1,500 people had died of those things in the flooded city as they were first abandoned and then attacked and prevented from evacuating and from receiving relief, died of stories that demonized and dehumanized them. And I'd fallen in love with what was most beautiful about New

Orleans, including the way that its inhabitants were good at being in the here and now, at being out in public and knowing where they were and celebrating in the streets and connecting with the people around them and at remembering the past that shaped this present. They had a talent for valuing other things more than productivity and efficiency, the miserable virtues that hustle people past each other and everyday attentiveness and pleasure.

That unhurriedness might be why a woman was confident she could hold up the long line to read my palm; I knew New Orleanians could take the delay in stride, and I let her take charge of my hand and override my own sense of obligation to keep things moving. I don't believe in palmistry or any other form of divination, but I believe in stories that come by any means, and in capacities strangers have to be messengers and mirrors in which you see new possibilities. Her parting words as she released my hand were, "Despite everything, you are who you were meant to be," and I kept them like a talisman.

Despite everything, she said, which I heard as the obstacles and injuries ordinary in billions of lives. I know how profoundly things have changed for the better, and how many people are nevertheless not who they were meant to be because the distorting mirror of gender gives them damaged senses of self, or because their rights and capacities or even conditions of survival are undermined. I cannot imagine a wholly undamaged human being or that that's a useful thing to imagine, though I can readily imagine that some of the kinds of damage inflicted on my gender can be reduced and delegitimized. I also think the process is under way, and that even being told that you deserve to be safe and free and equal can fortify you. If I'm both feminist and hopeful it's because I know how profoundly women's rights and status have changed, in many ways, in many places, since my birth.

Sylvia Plath at nineteen had mourned that "I want to talk to everybody I can as deeply as I can. I want to be able to sleep in an open field, to travel west, to walk freely at night" but she felt unable to because of her gender. I was born thirty years later and I and we have been more fortunate. I had roamed the West, slept in mountain meadows, in deserts, at the bottoms of canyons, on the banks of great rivers in the Southwest and the Arctic, driven vast distances alone, wandered many cities and some rural places at night, had organized with rebels, had blockaded streets, met heroes, written books, encouraged activists, had the friendships and conversations I yearned for when I was younger, had occasionally stood up for what I believed in, had stuck around long enough to see the arc of change across time in ways that were terrifying when it came to climate change and sometimes exhilarating when it came to cultural politics. Also it seems safe to say I'm damaged and a member of a society that damages us all and damages women in particular ways.

There are so many stories that can be told about damage. I ran across one in an essay on photographs of environmental destruction recently. The photographs showed the Carlin Trend, the belt of microscopic gold that runs through the Western Shoshone lands, including Carrie and Mary Dann's ranchlands, and that would have made Nevada, had it been an independent nation, the fourth or fifth biggest gold-producing country on earth. I'd visited the mines myself, enormous pits that could swallow cities, wounds out of which the water was pumped so that the gigantic equipment could keep going deeper, as whole mountains were pulverized and other heavy metals released, and cyanide-laced water poured through the dust to leach out the gold so that foreign corporations could reap a profit and people far away could ornament their bodies. The precious water of the desert was squandered, poisoned, then dumped into man-made lakes that killed the birds who landed in them. Knowing those mines made me hate gold.

The photographs came with an essay quoting another writer who'd worked for eight seasons in Antarctica. Jason C. Anthony wrote about the nutritional deficiencies common among sailors and polar explorers in the past and of their cause: "Without vitamin C, we cannot produce collagen, an essential component of bones, cartilage, tendons and other connective tissues. Collagen binds our wounds, but that binding is replaced continually throughout our lives. Thus in advanced scurvy, old wounds long thought healed will magically, painfully reappear."

You can read that as an insistence that we never get over anything, though it might make more sense as a reminder that though damage is not necessarily permanent, neither is repair. What is won or changed or fixed has to be maintained and protected or it can be lost. What goes forward can go backward. Efficiency says that grief should follow a road map and things should be gotten over and that then there should be that word that applies to wounds and minds both: *closure*. But time and pain are a more fluid, unpredictable business, expanding and contracting, closing and opening and changing.

You move toward or away from or around something that harmed you, or something or someone brings you back; that slippage in time, as though the stairs you exit on have become a waterfall, is the disorderliness of trauma and of trauma's sense of time. But sometimes you revisit the past, as I have in this book, to map the distance covered. There is closure and reopening and some-times something reopens because you can bring something new to it, repair it in a new way, by understanding it a new way. Sometimes the meaning of the beginning of the story has changed as new chap-ters are added.

Damage begets a different destiny than one you might have had otherwise, but it does not preclude having a life or making things that matter. Sometimes it's not despite but because of something terrible that you become who you are meant to be and set to the work you're meant to do. I heard "meant to be" not as though there was no damage but that it had not prevented me from doing what I was here to do. And some of my work was about that damage as it applied to so many of us. I've often wondered what people whose work is for justice and rights would've been in a world without the injustices, the lack of rights. Who would Martin Luther King Jr. have been in a nonracist society, Rachel Carson in an unpoisoned America? Unless you imagine them in a world without pain and harm, they might have found other wounds to try to heal. Paradise is often described as a place with nothing to do, nothing required of its inhabitants. I don't desire a paradise that demands nothing of us, and I see paradise as not a destination to arrive in, but a pole star by which to navigate.

The fortune-teller was a woman, and perhaps as women often do, as I often do, she only wanted to give me something to make me feel good, to make that microscopic utopia that is a moment of kind-ness, though even that a stranger wanted to give me a gift signifies. A few years ago, a man ran after me at the farmers' market and handed me a little hexagonal jar of honey from his stand; he had recognized me, though I'd never seen him before. To become a person that, occasionally, strangers want to reward because they felt I've given them something is an amazement. Once a young woman passing by an outdoor booth where I was signing books burst into a spontaneous jig at the sight of me, and that might be the pinnacle of my career, to be somehow an occasion for someone else's exuberance. We'd never set eyes on each other before, but that's the work that books do, reaching out further than their writers.

There's another story about wounds and repair that has captured a lot of imaginations in recent years. It's about the Japanese art of kintsugi, which literally means golden repair. It's a method of mending broken ceramic vessels with a bond made of powdered gold mixed with lacquer. The result turns the breaks into veins and channels of gold, emphasizing rather than hiding that the vessel has been broken and making it precious in another way than it was before. It's a way to accept that things will never be what they were but that they can become something else with a different kind of beauty and value. They are exquisite objects, these cups and bowls with their channels of gold like magical scars, like oracular patterns, road maps, hieroglyphs. They make me love gold.

My friend Roshi Joan Halifax, a feminist Buddhist leader, an anthropologist, and a constant traveler, has on several visits to Japan held these repaired vessels in her hands, and a few years ago, she explored them as a metaphor: "I am not suggesting that we should seek brokenness as a way of gaining strength, although some cultures do pursue crisis in their rites of passage as a way to strengthen character and open the heart," she wrote. "Rather, I am proposing that the wounds and harms that arise from falling over the edge into moral suffering can . . . be the means for the 'golden repair,' for developing a greater capacity to stand firm in our integrity without being swayed by the wind." And then my friend who had given me the desk sent me a letter to approve what I'd written about her that ended with a line from William Stafford: "I have woven a parachute out of everything broken."

People aren't really meant to be anything, because we're not made; we're born, with some innate tendencies, and thereafter molded, thwarted, scalded, encouraged by events and encounters. *Despite everything* suggests the forces that try to stop a person or change her nature and purpose, and *who you were meant to be* suggests that those forces did not altogether succeed. It was a lovely fortune to be handed by a stranger, and I took it, and with it the sense that who I was meant to be was a breaker of some stories and a maker of others, a tracer of the cracks and sometimes a repairwoman, and sometimes a porter or even a vessel for the most precious cargo you can carry, the stories waiting to be told, and the stories that set us free.

Acknowledgments

L ooking back, this is a book about obstacles and animosities, but also about bridge builders and kindnesses, and for the latter I owe so many thanks; to the latter I owe my survival. I'm here because of the forces that protect the vulnerable, encourage the eccentric, and educate the ignorant.

Thank you Mr. James V. Young (1920–1989) for a home and friendship.

Thank you, Western Addition, for an education in urbanism.

Thank you ____ for a desk to write on.

Thank you to the three main Davids of my twenties.

Thank you gay men, thank you queer culture, thank you city of refuge in those days when your principles were higher than your rents. Thank you City of San Francisco rent control policy, without which my trajectory would not have been possible.

Thank you Lyon-Martin Clinic for free health care for this straight kid in your queer-friendly spaces.

Thank you Ocean Beach, thank you Pacific, thank you fog-horns and seagulls. Thank you to the people who protected the vast greenbelt around San Francisco in which I have been wandering this past half century.

Thank you San Francisco Public Library and then UC Berkeley libraries for all the hours spent there and all the books and archives accessed there and the ideals you uphold. Thank you independent bookstores, especially Moe's, City Lights, Green Apple, Green Arcade, and all the bygone used bookstores.

Thank you San Francisco State University for making room for a transfer student and for schedules that that worked for working students; thank you Shakespeare professor Noel Wilson for encouragement and for getting me my first media job, as a fact-checker intern at *San Francisco Magazine*.

Thank you San Francisco Museum of Modern Art and the research/collections staff there and librarian Genie Candau. Thank you Sierra Club for thirty-five years of overlap and evolution.

Thank you Graduate School of Journalism, especially Bernard Taper, David Littlejohn, and Ben Bagdikian.

Thank you to the artists who taught me to think of myself as a writer, Linda Connor, Ann Hamilton, Richard Misrach, Lewis DeSoto, Meridel Rubenstein.

Thank you Gent Sturgeon and Rex Ray at City Lights and later on Paul Yamazaki there.

Thank you Rebecca Biggs, Steve Rosenberg, and Rob Langenbrunner, early publishers of mine in *Frank* magazine; thank you Tim Yohannon and *Maximum Rock'n'Roll*, ditto, thank you Flora at *Music Calendar*, Cecile McCann at *Artweek*, then Gary Kornblau at *Art issues*.

Thank you Bill Berkson, Michael McClure, and Barbara Stauffacher Solomon, early encouragers who came along when I was in my twenties, and Mike Davis and Lucy Lippard who showed up for me in my thirties.

Thank you to both my 1991 Gulf War and 2002–3 Iraq War Bay Area Direct Action Secret Society (BADASS) antiwar affinity groups.

Thank you to the handsome bikers at the Denny's on the I-5 north of Los Angeles who listened and let me convince them that Anita Hill was telling the truth, one morning at a shared table in October 1991.

Thank you Nevada: Bob Fulkerson, Carrie and Mary Dann, Corbin Harney, Chief Raymond Yowell, Bernice Lalo, Grace Potorti, Virginia/Dee-Dee Sanchez, Jo Anne Garrett, Marla Painter, Kaitlin Backlund, and my collaborators in the early version of the Western Shoshone Defense Project.

Thank you anti-intervention and environmental movements of the 1980s and Rainforest Action Network where I volunteered then (and where I met Brad Erickson of the Environmental Project on Central America, from whom I learned so much about environmental justice back then when he was learning it from Gwichin and Masaii elders); thank you antinuclear movement and Nevada Test Site activist friends of the 1990s; thank you climate activists of the twenty-first century among whom are so many friends and colleagues now, Bill and May and Anna and Joe and Steve and Mike B. and Antonia and Red.

Thank you Cleve Jones for that moment in 2018 when, because I showed up with the magnificent banner artist Stephanie Syjuco had made, you put me at the head of a march of gay men down our central boulevard, perhaps my greatest moment of arrival as a San Franciscan. Thank you for the democracy banner, Stephanie.

Thank you Garnette Cadogan, Elena Acevedo, and Jaime Cortez for friendship and insight and comments on this manuscript.

Thank you, six books later, Paul Slovak at Viking, my editor and encourager since he got the book proposal for *Wanderlust* in 1997. Thank you Penguin for first all the low-cost paperbacks that formed me and then for the glory of seeing my Viking hardcovers as Penguin paperbacks with the orange spines and Penguin logos. Thank you Bella Lacey and Pru Rowlandson at Granta.

Thank you Agent Frances Coady, encourager, first reader of this book.

Thank you to so many friends now—Marina, Astra, Sam, Leigh, Tina, Ana Teresa, Catherine—and especially to Charles, walking alongside me and sharing tea and more all through the writing of this book.

Thank you to all the women who have proved that stories can change the world, who have changed the collective story from the old overarching story built on endless silencing, thank you to the innumerable storytellers on social media, in public forums, in conversations, in the news, in books and courtrooms, who have broken that silence with their voices and made room thereby for other voices to be heard, perhaps before they too become survivors with terrible stories to tell.

Thank you feminism. Thank you intersections.

Here's to the liberation of all beings.

ALSO AVAILABLE

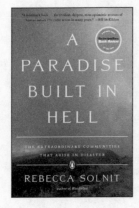  

THE FARAWAY NEARBY

A PARADISE BUILT IN HELL
The Extraordinary Communities That Arise in Disaster

A FIELD GUIDE TO GETTING LOST

RIVER OF SHADOWS
Eadweard Muybridge and the Technological Wild West

WANDERLUST
A History of Walking

(P) PENGUIN BOOKS

Ready to find your next great read? Let us help. Visit prh.com/nextread